CW01367236

STACK 6. DEC. 2002

27. 01. 06.

2 3 NOV ....

23. 10. 02

13.11.02
TH.

CHURCH, Peter Campbell

Focus on Southeast Asia

400000008   £11.95

Please return/renew this item by the last date shown
Thank you for using your local library

BARNSLEY LIBRARIES

BARNSLEY LIBRARIES

3 8059 40000 0008

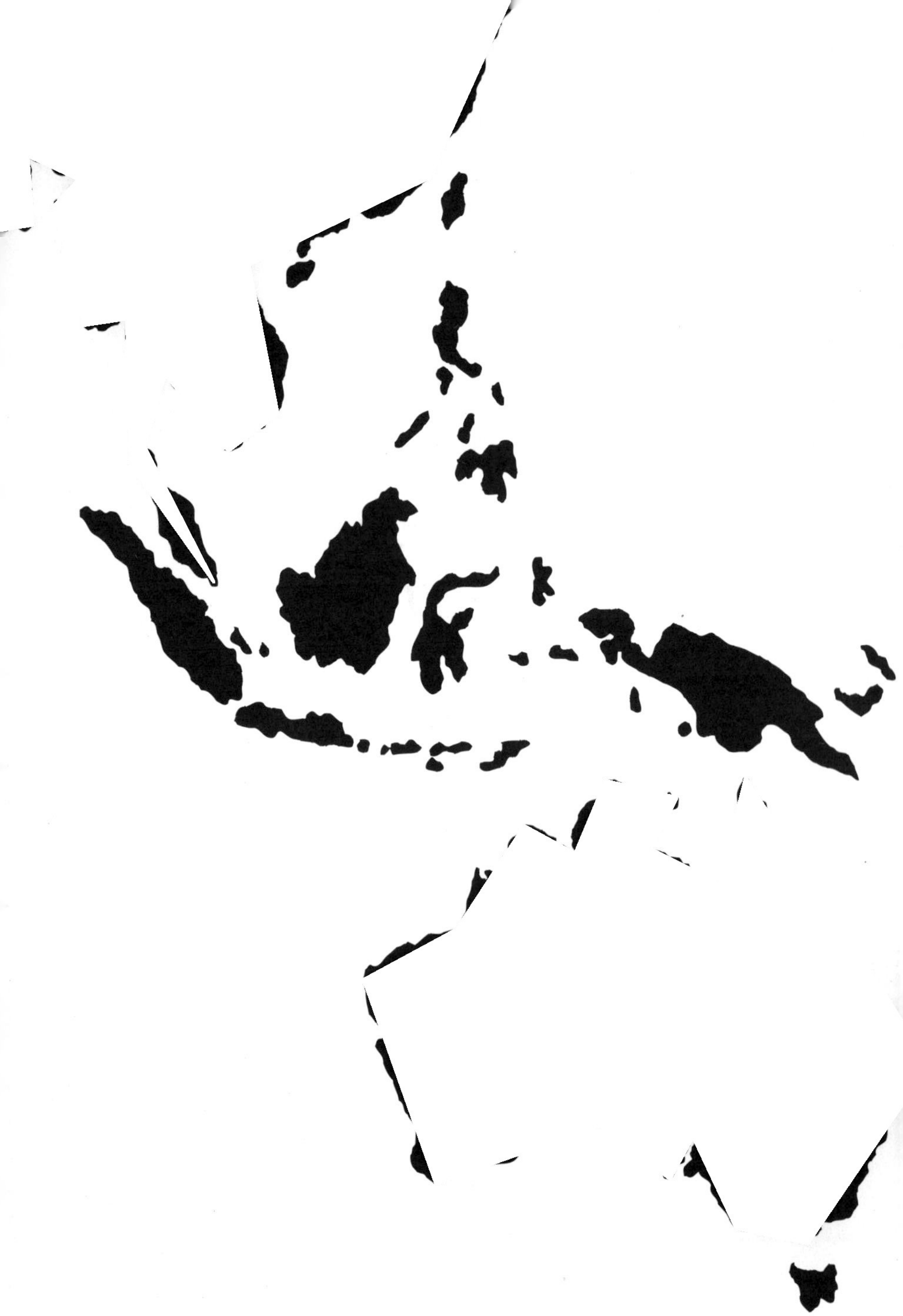

Focus on Southeast Asia

ASEAN FOCUS GROUP

Edited by Peter Church
ALLEN & UNWIN

Copyright © Asean Focus Group (Hong Kong) 1995

All rights reserved. No part of this book may be reproduced or transmitted in any form or by any means, electronic or mechanical, including photocopying, recording or by any information storage and retrieval system, without prior permission in writing from the publisher.

First published in 1995 by
Allen & Unwin Pty Ltd
9 Atchison Street, St Leonards, NSW 2065 Australia

National Library of Australia
Cataloguing-in-Publication entry:

Focus on Southeast Asia.

   Bibliography.
   ISBN 1 86373 940 8.

   1. Asia, Southeastern – History. 2. Asia, Southeastern – Civilisation. I. Church, Peter (Peter C.).

959

Designed and typeset in 10pt Times Roman by Roy Blinston
Printed by KHL Printing Co Pte Ltd, Singapore

10 9 8 7 6 5 4 3 2 1

Contents

Foreword 7

The Region 8

Brunei 12

Cambodia 20

Indonesia 38

Lao PDR 54

Malaysia 66

Myanmar 86

Philippines 98

Singapore 112

Thailand 124

Vietnam 142

Further Reading 156

Maps 161

About the Asean Focus Group 171

*'to understand
the present and anticipate
the future, one must
know enough of
the past,
enough to have
a sense of the
history of a people'*

Lee Kuan Yew,
then Prime Minister of Singapore,
on the occasion of the
25th anniversary of the founding of
the People's Action Party
in January 1980

Foreword

I had already been involved with Southeast Asia for many years when I read the former Prime Minister of Singapore, Lee Kuan Yew's thought-provoking words. Although I was an indifferent student of history at school in Australia, the words hit me like a sledge hammer. Whilst I was well aware of the importance to business of understanding the different cultures of Southeast Asia, I had not given a lot of thought to the relevance of history to the future in general, or to business in particular.

Since that time I have read a lot of history on the region and what I have learnt has over and over again reinforced Lee Kuan Yew's message. Unfortunately, I have found much of the history of the region has either been written by scholars absorbed by their topics and writing at a much greater depth than is required to get that broad understanding of the history of the people or has been written in an abbreviated form for tourists or others needing only an outline of the past.

This book is our first attempt to find a middle path which will give business and other readers enough detail to have a sense of the history of the different countries and their people. In so doing, we engaged the assistance of two leading Australian historians who specialise in the Asean region, Professor John Ingleson and Dr Ian Black of the University of New South Wales. They immediately understood what it was that we were trying to achieve and through their skill, sensitivity and experience the first drafts of this book were produced. Our chairman, Rawdon Dalrymple, a former Ambassador to Indonesia, the United States and Japan, also contributed significantly, including a regional overview.

The project proved to be a far more difficult exercise than at first envisaged. Not only is it difficult to condense thousands of years of history to a few pages but, at all times, we wanted to test the material against the objective that a reader should by the end of each chapter have a feel for the history of the particular people.

Above all, we hope you come away from reading our book with a deeper understanding of the history of Southeast Asia which might, in a small way, better enable you to understand the present and interpret the future with respect to your Southeast Asian business and other interests.

PETER C. CHURCH, OAM
Managing Director, Asean Focus Group

Sydney, 15 March 1995

The Region

This book was written to give readers convenient, informative and expert summaries of the histories of the countries of Southeast Asia. For visitors, particularly business people, such information is increasingly necessary as they become involved in one way or another with these countries which are rapidly assuming much greater importance in today's world.

It was not part of our purpose to address the regional picture as such or the way in which these countries have interacted with each other. But as they become larger, economically stronger and more confident of their actual and potential influence, their relations with each other and with the rest of the world will be increasingly important. The Southeast Asians are likely to play a far larger role in the world in the coming decades than they have in the past. Their cooperation with each other and their growing awareness that they have strengths which are different from those of the West will be central to that process.

The post–Cold War world is seeing in some areas a resurgence of nationalism and in others a greater emphasis on regionalism. These two tendencies will overlap. In Southeast Asia national and ethnic differences were significantly blunted by European colonialism and in some cases have been further submerged in the post–colonial period of new nation states. But what is new in Southeast Asia is the development of voluntary (as distinct from externally mandated) cooperation on a sub-regional or regional level. Most recently there is the assertion of an Asian identity, shared by Southeast Asians, which is sharply distinguished from Western value systems, social norms and economic models. It is too early to say how far that will be taken or how much it will influence the political and social development of Southeast Asia. The very important differences between and indeed even within the Southeast Asian countries induce some scepticism in academic circles about the existence of 'Asian values' etc. But there is no doubt that there is a perception in the region of some essential shared values or priorities, and a rejection of what are seen as Western individualistic and libertarian values.

An embryonic sense of shared interests transcending ethnic or national groups emerged in colonial times between independence movements, student movements and other groups, including notably the various Marxist-inspired or communist movements in the region.

But until after the Pacific War there was little connection across the region. The colonial empires were very separate and governed on different principles.

It is a common observation nowadays that Australia, on the fringe of the region, only recently and belatedly become aware of and involved with its Southeast Asian neighbours. That is true, though with some qualifications. There was peripheral contact in the north even before the Europeans colonised

Australia. But in the colonial era there was no steady development of contact or interest. The shifting patterns of alliance politics in Europe affected such contacts as there were between the colonial administrations in Southeast Asia and Australia, and indeed between the Southeast Asian colonial administrations themselves.

Australia was not unique, or even unusual, in having little contact with its neighbours and in having its external links directed principally along the lines laid down by the metropolitan power. What are now the independent nations of Southeast Asia also had little contact with each other during the European colonial period. Just as the lines of communication and trade ran from Melbourne and Sydney to London, so did those between the French, Dutch, and other British colonies and the respective metropolitan powers in Europe.

Right up to the Pacific War there was little or no communication between, for example, what are now Indonesia, Vietnam, Malaysia, and the Philippines. The links ran from Manila to the United States, from Batavia to the Netherlands, from Hanoi to France, and so on.

It was the remarkable Japanese campaign which began at the end of 1941 which precipitated or accelerated the radical changes which took place between 1945 and the end of the Vietnam War. The sheer speed and success of the Japanese successes against numerically superior defending forces in Southeast Asia made a strong impression on opinion in the erstwhile colonies.

The Japanese failed to capitalise on that in the sense that after early political successes in encouraging nationalist and pro-Japanese movements the appeal to shared Asian interests lost plausibility in the face of Japanese policies and actions which were exploitative or worse.

Although Japan lost the war and left wounds in the region which are still not healed, the war precipitated the end of the moribund European colonial era, and accelerated the creation of independent states largely within borders established by the colonial empires. For some years trade and other economic links remained predominantly in the old colonial grooves. Then the economic supremacy of the United States and Japan's decades of explosive economic growth caused those patterns to diversify.

In the region the United States and Japan became the two most important outside powers and that was reflected inter alia by their leading roles in the setting up of the Asian Development Bank in 1966. By that time Australia too had perforce diversified its trade away from Britain which had made it clear that it would seek its future economic arrangements in Europe and the Commonwealth arrangements which had supported much of Australia's traditional export industry were phased out. Australia turned to Japan and others for new markets (a trade agreement with Japan had already been made in 1957).

Australia's development assistance programme had from the beginning concentrated on Southeast Asia and became an increasingly important instrument for involving this country with the region, especially as significant numbers of students from the region came to our universities and other institutions under the Colombo Plan and successor programmes.

The failure of the attempted coup in Indonesia, the Gestapu of 30 September 1965, and the subsequent establishment of the New Order government there, opened the way to overcome the regional or sub-regional strains produced by President Sukarno's efforts to crush the newly-constructed Malaysia, as well as other tensions created or exacerbated by the Sukarno policies.

In this climate ASEAN, the Association of South East Asian Nations, was established in 1967 and set out on its long and successful course of gradually building a sense of common interest and regional association among the six (originally five) members. ASEAN recently embarked on the development of AFTA, the ASEAN Free Trade Agreement.

ASEAN has become the key institution in Southeast Asia not only because of its success in developing a sense of community among its very disparate members, and in finding a road for them to closer economic cooperation. It has also become the forum for discussion with the main world powers on a wide range of matters. This has come about through an annual mechanism of post–Ministerial consultations held after ASEAN's own internal consultations through which ASEAN member governments, at Foreign Minister level, meet with their counterparts. These counterparts, termed 'dialogue partners', currently are Australia, Canada, the European Union, Japan, the Republic of Korea, New Zealand and the United States. In 1994 discussions on regional security were further developed with the establishment of the ASEAN Regional Forum (ARF) which groups ASEAN and its dialogue partners with Russia, China, Vietnam, Lao and Papua New Guinea.

Looking at the recent evolution of Southeast Asia perhaps the most significant thing has been the change that has occurred since the ending of the Cold War and the collapse of communism. Until relatively recently the centrally planned economy model had much attraction for many developing countries and there was up to the beginning of the eighties quite widespread aversion to capitalism and to the liberal market model as exemplified by the Western industrialised countries.

Now virtually all of Southeast Asia is committed to market economics, albeit with more governmental political control than in the Western countries. There is a virtual unanimity about the commitment to economic development based on relatively open markets, private ownership and competition. With that has come a period of unprecedented economic growth. The major economies of Southeast Asia are all growing at rates previously thought unattainable for a sustained period. There are of course some uncertainties about the future; but there are few who doubt that Southeast Asia will early in the twenty-first century be a major centre of economic power and influence.

The following country chapters should therefore be read with the sense that they are building blocks in an overall picture. They are essential elements in an understanding of Southeast Asia. The development of regional awareness and cooperation which I have briefly discussed here is quite recent. But it seems to be gathering strength and to have great potential to affect for good or ill the course of Southeast Asia's history.

TIMELINES

1987: Brunei joins ASEAN

1984: Brunei becomes a sovereign state

1962: State of Emergency declared after first and only elections held

1959: Self government

1920: Oil and natural gas discovered

1888: Britain declares Brunei a protectorate

1839: James Brooke arrives and becomes the Governor and 'White Rajah' of Sarawak (then part of Brunei)

18th century: Brunei's area of economic and political influence gradually declines

16th-17th centuries: Brunei becomes a major regional Kingdom extending to southern Philippines, Sabah and Sarawak

1521: Magellan visits a flourishing trading community linked to Southeast Asia and China

14th century: Brunei claimed as part of the Majapahit Empire

6th-9th centuries: Kingdom of Puni on the northwest coast of Kalimantan paying tribute to China

ASEAN FOCUS GROUP

Brunei

Brunei Darussalam (Brunei) is a small state of just 5,765 square kilometers located on the north-west coast of the island of Kalimantan, or 'Borneo' (a western term derived from 'Brunei'). It is an Islamic State where the Sultan, Sir Hassanal Bolkiah, the twenty-ninth in the dynasty, rules by decree. Its population is about 280,000, of whom nearly 60 per cent live in urban areas. Malays make up about 64 per cent of the population, Chinese about 20 per cent and indigenous tribes about 8 per cent. It would be an unremarkable territory were it not that underneath its soil and under its territorial waters lie huge oil and gas reserves which have enabled the country to have the highest per capita income in Southeast Asia. This underground wealth has also enabled one of the world's few remaining absolute monarchies to survive to the end of the 20th century. The Sultanate has considerable financial reserves invested throughout the world.

Early History

Little is known of the early history of Brunei. There appears to have been trade between the north-west coast of Kalimantan and China as early as the 6th century and Brunei was influenced by the spread of Hinduism/Buddhism from India in the first millenium. Chinese records make mention of a kingdom of Puni, located on the north-west coast of Kalimantan, which paid tribute to Chinese emperors between the 6th and the 9th centuries. Brunei was claimed by the great Javanese empire of Majapahit in the 14th century, though it was most likely little more than a trading/tributary relationship. Brunei became a more significant state in the 15th century with a greater degree of independence from its larger neighbours. When the Chinese Admiral Cheng Ho visited Brunei in the early 15th century, as part of his exploration of Southeast Asia, he discovered a significant trading port with resident Chinese traders engaged in profitable trade with the homeland.

Brunei was a small cog in the early Southeast trading networks but well enough known to figure in the records of the major states. The Brunei ruler seems to have converted to Islam in the middle of the 15th century when he married a daughter of the ruler of Melaka (now Malacca in Peninsular Malaysia). The Portuguese conquest of Melaka in 1511 closed it to Muslim traders, forcing them to look elsewhere.

There was an outflow of wealthy Islamic traders who settled in other parts of the Indonesian archipelago taking with them not only their business acumen but also their religious beliefs. The Islamisation of the region was given a great impetus. Brunei prospered from the Portuguese conquest of Melaka as Islamic traders were now attracted to its port in greater numbers. When Magellan's expedition visited Brunei in 1521 it found a prosperous town with a flourishing trading community linked into the Southeast Asia–China trading network. Throughout the 16th century it engaged in political and commercial relations with other states in the Malay world, comprising the Indonesian archipelago, the Malay peninsula and the southern Philippines.

Brunei became a major regional kingdom in the 16th and 17th centuries, with its influence stretching into the southern Philippines and its territorial claims extending over most of the north coast of Kalimantan, including what are now the Malaysian states of Sarawak and Sabah. As the first Islamic kingdom in the area Brunei was the base for the Islamisation of the southern Philippines and surrounding areas, frequently coming into conflict with Catholic Spain after the Spanish conquest of Luzon, the central island of the Philippines. In 1578 Spain attacked Brunei and briefly captured the capital. It was unable to hold the town, largely because its forces were decimated by sickness. Spain continued to try to conquer the Islamic Sultanate of Sulu in the southern Philippine islands, finally succeeding in the last quarter of the nineteenth century.

Brunei did well out of the Portuguese conquest of Melaka. Not only did it become an important port for Muslim traders but it was able to negotiate a deal with the Portuguese for cooperation in the Southeast Asian trade with China. Brunei was no threat to Portugal, having no territorial claims outside Kalimantan. It also shared a commercial interest in promoting the China trade. In 1526 the Portuguese established a trading post at Brunei to collect the valued products of Kalimantan and surrounding islands. Brunei became an integral port of call on the Melaka to Macau route.

Brunei's commercial and political power was at its peak in the middle of the seventeenth century. It had managed to stave off Spain and had reached a mutually beneficial accord with Portugal. From the middle of the 17th century it was increasingly challenged by the Sultanate of Sulu in the islands north-east of Kalimantan. Ostensibly under Brunei sovereignty, the Sultanate of Sulu gradually established total independence, going so far as to acquire from Brunei sovereignty over most of the area which today constitutes the Malaysian State of Sabah.

By the beginning of the 18th century the political and economic power of the Malay rulers in Kalimantan and what is now the southern Philippines was declining sharply. The rule of the once-powerful Sultans of Brunei and Sulu now barely extended outside their capitals. Their decline resulted largely from the development of European entrepots in Southeast Asia, which offered local traders a better price for their produce and were free from the taxes of the Malay ports. The development of local trade with European entrepots, especially Singapore, Batavia (Jakarta) and Manila, and the decay of the older trading centres of Brunei and Sulu meant a drastic reduction in the Sultanates' revenues with a consequent decline in political power.

About 40,000 people lived in Brunei town and surrounding areas in the mid-eighteenth century. By the 1830s the population had declined to about 10,000. The northern coast of Kalimantan, except for Brunei town itself, was ruled by local chiefs based at river mouths. The coastal population was predominantly Malay (and Muslim) with a small group of Chinese merchants and pepper growers and a smattering of people of Arab descent. The tribal people who lived in the interior were neither Malay nor Muslim: they were subsistence farmers who traded with the coastal Malays but resisted attempts to bring them under Malay control. To Brunei's west (in Sarawak) the most significant tribal people were Iban, or Dayak. To the east (in Sabah) the most significant groups were Kadazan–Dusun and Murut.

In addition to its economic decay the Brunei Sultanate was further weakened by power struggles within the Court. Omar Ali Saifuddin, who succeeded to the throne of the Sultanate in 1828, was a weak ruler. During his reign a bitter power struggle developed between two rival factions led by Brunei Chiefs. The decline in the Sultan's power was evidenced by the increasing independence of provincial rulers, and by the growth in the power of formerly subservient chiefs. In the late 1830s, Sarawak, the westernmost province claimed by the Sultanate of Brunei, was in open rebellion against the local provincial ruler whose rule had become progressively more oppressive as he became more independent of Brunei. In 1837 the Sultan tried to suppress the rebellion but without success.

The British impact

In the first half of the 19th century the interest of the British government and the English East India Company in Southeast Asia was limited to the protection of the China trade routes from interference by other European nations and the provision of minimum conditions for the expansion of British trade in the area. The Anglo–Dutch Treaty of 1824, under which Britain acquired Melaka from the Dutch and relinquished Benkulen on the south-west coast of Sumatra and under which the Dutch withdrew all objections to Britain's occupation of Singapore, contained articles which guaranteed British traders' entry to the Dutch-administered ports and laid down maximum rates of import duties.

The failure of the Dutch to carry out the commercial clauses of the Treaty led to a growing agitation by merchants in Singapore and Britain that Britain should directly challenge the Netherland's position in the Archipelago by opening an entrepot to the east of Singapore. The unsuccessful settlements in northern Australia – Melville Bay, Raffles Bay and Port Essington – had been made partly with this end in view, but in the late 1830s attention was focused on the north-west coast of Borneo, the only part of the Archipelago not recognised as lying within the Dutch sphere of influence.

Into this situation of a decaying Sultanate of Brunei, facing rebellion in Sarawak and a growing commercial interest in the north-west coast of Kalimantan by the British community in Singapore, a remarkable Englishman named James Brooke arrived in August 1839. Brooke was in the mould of the early 19th century Romantics: he admired what he saw as the simple and unsophisticated life of the peoples of the Malay Archipelago and wanted to improve it by bringing to them what he saw as the benefits of British civilisation, without destroying the basic simplicity of their lives. He became convinced that he had a divinely-appointed mission in the Malay archipelago. With the proceeds of his wealthy father's estate he bought a boat and journeyed first to Singapore and then to the north-west coast of Kalimantan. His timely arrival at the head of the Sarawak river with an armed yacht in August 1839 brought the rebellion of the local chief to an end. In return he received the Governorship of Sarawak.

Over the next thirty years Brooke established a personal fiefdom in Sarawak, remorselessly extending its borders at the expense of the Sultanate of Brunei. He was adroit at persuading British naval commanders in Hong Kong and Singapore to support him in forcing the Sultan of Brunei to make concession after concession. However, his attempts to persuade the British government to make Sarawak a British protectorate for the moment fell on deaf ears. The 'White Rajah' was one of the more colourful oddities in the history of British colonialism.

A weakened Sultan of Brunei made further concessions of territory in 1877. This time it was to a private company, the American Trading Company, owned by an Austrian and an Englishman. The Austrian sold out to the Englishman in 1881. In order to keep the French and the Germans out of a strategically important area, Britain then granted a royal charter for the establishment of the British North Borneo Company. Further Brunei territory was successfully claimed by Sarawak in 1882, reducing the Sultanate to two small areas, the core around Brunei town and a small pocket of land inside Sarawak. In 1888 in order to protect what was left of the once great Sultanate of Brunei and finally to ensure that rival European powers were kept out, Britain declared a protectorate over Sarawak, Brunei and North Borneo. A series of arrangements between the British North Borneo Company and Sarawak saw Sarawak add further territory and in 1906 Britain appointed a Resident to Brunei in order to supervise the state, modernise its administrative structures and ensure its survival against its predatory Sarawak neighbour.

Brunei had been territorially reduced to but a shadow of its former self. But oil and gas were discovered beneath its land and under its territorial waters in the 1920s. The history of Brunei from then on has revolved around the enormous wealth created by oil and gas. The Sultan and his family became very rich, very quickly. Access to such a strong revenue stream enabled the Sultanate by the 1960s to provide free health, education and social welfare services of a high standard to all its people, and all with very low rates of taxation.

After the Second World War and the defeat of Japan, Brunei continued to be a British protectorate with the Sultan ruling with advice from a British Resident and under the protection of Gurkha troops. As Britain steadily decolonised in Asia and Africa, this arrangement came to be seen in Britain as anachronistic. In 1959 Brunei achieved self-government, at the insistence of Britain. A constitution was drawn up which provided for elections to a legislative council. In 1962 the first elections were held. They were won by the Party Rakyat Brunei, a party which opposed the monarchical system and demanded full democratic rights. It also advocated that Brunei join the neighbouring states of Sabah and Sarawak in the mooted Federation of Malaysia. The Partai Rakyat Brunei was strongly opposed by the Sultan and the ruling elite and its demands were rejected. Brunei was to remain a monarchy.

As a consequence the Partai Rakyat Brunei launched a revolt which was quickly crushed by the Gurkha troops stationed in Brunei. The Sultan declared a state of emergency, suspended the constitution, declared the recent elections void and banned the Partai Rakyat Brunei. This was the only election ever held in Brunei. In 1962 and early 1963 the Sultan became involved in discussions about joining the new Federation of Malaysia, but when Malaysia was formed in September 1963 Brunei elected to remain outside. Disagreements over the distribution of oil and gas revenues (Brunei was determined to protect its revenue) and concern about the relative status of the royal family among the other Malaysian Sultans, all of whom were constitutional monarchs with limited powers, finally persuaded the then Sultan, that Brunei should remain a British protectorate.

The protectorate arrangements were changed in 1971, but Britain still retained control of foreign affairs and defence, although all costs were now met by a very wealthy Sultanate. At Britain's insistence, embarrassed by the continuation of this relic of colonialism, Brunei became a sovereign state on 1 January 1984. Independence brought with it few perceptible changes for the people of Brunei. Political parties remain banned. State ministries essentially remain in the hands of members of the royal family and trusted members of a tightly knit elite.

Since the 1960s, Brunei has become increasingly involved with its Southeast Asian neighbours. Its relations with the countries making up ASEAN (originally Indonesia, Malaysia, the Philippines, Singapore and Thailand) since its formation in 1967 have been extremely good, although from time to time there has been some debate in sections of Malaysian society about the merits of Brunei's benevolent but authoritarian monarchy. In 1987 Brunei joined Asean as a full member, thereby formalising the already close relationship.

Brunei's revenues are almost entirely dependent on royalties from oil and gas. Conscious of the eventual exhaustion of these finite resources, the Brunei Government in the 1980s and 1990s has placed priority on developing the agricultural sector so that it can cease to be a net importer of food. Efforts are also being made to develop light manufacturing. But for the foreseeable future Brunei will be dependent on oil and gas revenues and the considerable income from its investments overseas.

The social composition of Brunei has changed quickly over the past four decades, most noticeably in the growth of an educated middle class. This educated middle class will contiue to increase in numbers. A major question is the extent to which the middle class will demand greater political involvement and representation in keeping with their educational and economic achievements.

TIMELINES

1993: Royal Government of Cambodia

1991-93: United Nations Transitional Authority in Cambodia (UNTAC)

1979: Vietnamese forces invade and take control from the Khmer Rouge

1975-79: Democratic Kampuchea under control of Khmer Rouge

1970: Khmer Republic proclaimed

1955: Norodom Sihanouk elected and period of 'Buddhist Socialism' begins

1953: Independence granted

1863: Treaty with France marks start of colonial period

1845: Thailand and Vietnam compromise and Cambodia pays homage to both countries

17th-18th centuries: Repeated incursions by Thailand and Vietnam

1593: Thailand invades and Cambodia becomes part of the Kingdom of Ayudhya

9th-14th centuries: Angkor Kingdom

3rd-7th centuries: Funan society covering southern Myanmar, Thailand, Cambodia and southern Vietnam

Cambodia

No country in Southeast Asia has a more imposing early history than Cambodia. The temples of Angkor, erected between the 9th and 13th centuries, still testify to the creative energy, wealth and power of Khmer society in that era. But no country in the region has a more tragic present. Ravaged by war and revolution in the 1970s, a decade in which more than one in seven Cambodians died, Cambodia remained a victim of international Cold War rivalries in the 1980s. Today peace and even the most elementary economic security cannot be guaranteed in Cambodia.

One striking theme in Cambodia's history is the country's almost continuous entrapment in the rivalries of outside forces. Until the 19th century these forces were regional. Since then Cambodia has been tossed and tormented by world forces, to a degree that sometimes seems inexplicable given Cambodia's small population and poverty. Cambodia's population was assessed at 9.27 million in 1993 with a GDP per capita of less than US$200.

Another striking historical theme, intertwined with the first, concerns the perennial struggles for power within Cambodia at the expense of the country's general well being. Traditionally a matter of ruling class rivalries, the power struggles have been grotesquely magnified by this century's global ideological collisions. Cambodia has known peace, sometimes for extended periods, but always under rulers who enforced peace. French colonial rule achieved a kind of peace in Cambodia, as did King Sihanouk in the 1950s and 1960s. Today an internationally-backed Cambodian government is again trying to enforce peace. It remains to be seen if this government can achieve peace, and for how long.

Early history and the empire of Angkor

The first glimpses into Cambodian history come from the early centuries of the Christian era. By then Khmers – direct ancestors of Cambodia's modern population – and related Mon peoples occupied a broad band of mainland Southeast Asia, stretching across what is today southern Burma, Thailand, Cambodia and southern Vietnam. Early Chinese records mention trade with a society on the lower Mekong which they term 'Funan' (perhaps a transcription of the Khmer word Phnom, meaning hill).

Funan flourished from the 3rd to 7th centuries, a port of call on the sea-trading route between India and China. Its Hindu-Buddhist religious life, writing system, irrigation technology for wet rice-growing and other skills were probably developed from Indian sources. Families claiming high Brahman status became a feature of Khmer society, providing priests for Hindu rituals and senior officials for Khmer rulers.

Khmer society did not adopt the caste system of Indian Hindu society, but it did become strongly hierarchical in structure.

The Chinese records mention two other early societies in the Khmer area – 'water Chenla' in the Mekong delta and 'land Chenla' further up the Mekong, possibly in what is now southern Lao. The records indicate that the latter attacked Funan, bringing about its demise. However the evidence is inadequate to know whether the two 'Chenlas' and indeed Funan were coherent states, or rather loose collections of farming and trading communities under warlords – albeit warlords aspiring to be seen as divinely-ordained warrior kings, identified with Hindu deities such as Siva and Vishnu.

The consolidation of Khmer society is more clear from the 9th century, when the first of the kings to rule over the state now generally known as Angkor, Jayavarman II (who reigned from around 802–850), established the state cult of Devaraj, or 'god-king'. This cult, while incorporating Khmer animist beliefs, centred on the worship of a linga relating the king to Siva and symbolising the king's ability to confer fertility and prosperity on his land and people. A temple built to house the linga represented the mythical Mount Meru, centre of the universe and home of the gods. Thus the king was identified with the divine world, and could lay claim to universal authority. At the king's death his temple could serve as his mausoleum.

Jayavarman II built several such temples at widely spaced sites in what is now Cambodia. For the next four centuries his successors would build their temple-mausoleums, the successive foci of Southeast Asia's greatest state until the 13th century. The temples of the Angkor region together with Borobudur in Java and Bagan (Pagan) in Myanmar, are still amongst Southeast Asia's most imposing historical remains.

From the mid-9th century Angkor's heartland became the region along the northern end of the Tonle Sap, near the modern city of Siem Reap. The Tonle Sap ('great lake') floods each year, fed by the rushing waters of the Mekong. Angkor's rulers and people gradually built a system of reservoirs and canals to control the inundation and provide year-round water for multiple rice harvests. The system eventually watered an area of about 5.5 million hectares and supported a large population. A 'bureaucracy' of regional magnates and officials harnessed the labour and product of this population for the king's projects and their own – temple-building, the lavish decoration and upkeep of temples and palaces, the expansion and maintenance of the irrigation works, trade with merchants sailing up the Mekong/Tonle Sap, and warfare.

The degree of power personally exercised by the 'god-kings' remains uncertain, despite the rich information about Angkor provided by temple inscriptions and bas-reliefs. Modern scholars' characterisations of Angkor's rulers vary from Stalinesque tyrants to ceremonial figureheads always in danger from court rivalries and regional challenges. Two men of immensely strong personality stand out from the long line of monarchs – Suryavarman II (reigned 1113–1150) and Jayavarman VII (reigned 1181–1219). The former took the empire which Angkor had been developing to its greatest extent. Under him it encompassed much of modern Thailand and Lao, Cambodia and southern Vietnam. For a time he also held the territory of Champa (today central Vietnam). Appropriately, Suryavarman II initiated the construction of Angkor Wat, sometimes termed the largest religious building in the world, and Angkor's best known monument.

Jayavarman VII, also a triumphant warrior-king, became the most prolific of all Angkor's royal builders. His greatest monument is the massive Angkor Thom and Bayon but he also established numerous other temples, all in an apparent attempt to promote a form of Mahayana Buddhism. He also initiated a road-building program plus other public works such as hospitals and rest-houses. The mobilisation of labour and resources for warfare and building during the reign of Jayavarman VII must have been enormous. Following his death early in the 13th century no more temples were built and the incising of inscriptions also ceased. Most commentators suggest that his fearsome energies brought social exhaustion. Nevertheless the next major insight into Angkor available to us – the account of a Chinese visitor, Chou Ta-kuan, in 1296 – suggests a state still of great power and opulence.

By then, however, the principal religious focus of Khmer society had altered. Varieties of Buddhism had long coexisted with the Hindu Devaraj cults but, during the 13th century, Theravada Buddhism won general allegiance. This form of Buddhism, originally defined in Sri Lanka and possibly Burma, was relatively strongly organised by its sangha (order of monks) and clear about what constituted Buddhist orthodoxy, while also being able to subsume Hindu and animist elements. It was rapidly becoming the dominant religion in mainland Southeast Asia. The concept of Devaraj, celebrated by Brahmanic officials, would persist in Khmer society, but a godly king would now demonstrate his virtue primarily through patronage of Theravada Buddhist temples, monasteries and schools. As a consequence, perhaps, interest in the temple-mausoleums of former rulers declined.

In the 1440s the Khmer ruling class abandoned the Angkor region. Besides the impact of Theravada Buddhism there are other possible reasons for this shift. Court factionalism may have weakened the firm government needed for such an intricately connected 'hydraulic society' to work, and hastened ecological deterioration of a region intensively exploited for centuries.

The general population of the area may have drifted away as the irrigation system silted up. Malaria has also been suggested as a factor in Angkor's abandonment. The best established factor in the transfer of the kingdom is the rise from 1351 of the ambitious Thai state of Ayudhya. The Thais consistently attacked Angkor, looting it of wealth and people. A Khmer capital to the southeast (variously in later centuries Phnom Penh, Udong and Lovek) may have seemed more defensible than Angkor. Such cities were also nearer the sea and the booming maritime trade of 15th century Southeast Asia.

The kingdom of Cambodia, 16th–18th centuries

Until late in the 16th century the translated Khmer kingdom appears to have been quite strong, an equal of neighbours like Ayudhya, Lan Xang (Lao) and Vietnam. Intermittent warfare with the Thais continued, but so did peaceable trade and cultural exchange. In religion, polity and culture the Thai and Khmer kingdoms had much in common. In 1593, however, the Thai king Narasuen attacked Cambodia as part of his strategy to reaffirm the power of Ayudhya after a devastating assault on his city by the Burmese. From this time Cambodia slipped decisively – at least in Thai eyes – to the status of a Thai vassal state.

Shortly after Narasuen's attack Cambodia demonstrated vividly a feature that would darken its history in the centuries ahead – ruling class attempts to harness foreign assistance in ruling class rivalries. In the 1590s aid was sought from the Spanish, by then ensconced at Manila, against the Thais. Spanish adventurers and missionaries briefly held great influence at the Cambodian court but in 1599 most were massacred. The king who had favoured them was assassinated. In 1603, after further upheavals at court, a Cambodian prince aligned with the Thais came to the throne.

Meanwhile, the Vietnamese had long been advancing southwards from their original homeland in the Tonkin delta, overwhelming Champa in the process. In the 1620s the next Cambodian king turned to the Vietnamese for help against the Thais, permitting Vietnamese settlement along his kingdom's southeast coast. There the Vietnamese port and stronghold of Saigon would develop. Vietnamese and Chinese adventurers and traders began to dominate other Cambodian ports. European accounts of Cambodia in the late 16th century and first half of the 17th century suggest a cosmopolitan trading life involving Chinese, Japanese, Malay, Arab and other traders, but from the mid-17th century Cambodia became increasingly isolated from the sea, caught in the pincer movement of Thai and Vietnamese expansionism.

The later 17th and 18th centuries saw repeated Thai and Vietnamese incursions, usually connected with rivalries for the throne within the Cambodian ruling class. The 18th century ended with the Thais dominant.

From 1771 until the early 19th century the Vietnamese were preoccupied with domestic rebellion and civil war. The Thai General Taksin and the Thai ruler Rama I, the founder of Bangkok, took the opportunity to impose their authority firmly over Cambodia. The northwestern provinces of Battambang and Siem Reap were added to Thai territory. The Cambodian kings had their subordinate status made plain by being crowned at Bangkok amidst Thai-dictated ceremonies.

But Thai-Vietnamese rivalry was still to climax. The Cambodian ruler Ang Chan (reigned 1806–35) thought it wise to pay homage not only to the Thais but also to the Vietnamese, by now reunited under a strong new dynasty ruling from the city of Hué. In 1811–12 Thai forces attempted to replace Ang Chan with one of his brothers, but Vietnamese troops repelled the Thais, and Vietnam assumed ascendancy over Cambodia. Ang Chan continued, however, to send tribute to Bangkok as well as to Hué.

In 1833 the Thais staged a major invasion, taking Phnom Penh, but they were again repelled by Vietnamese forces. When Ang Chan died in 1834 the Vietnamese emperor Minh Mang decided on a policy of complete absorption of Cambodia within his realm. As a first step he passed over two male heirs of the late king and appointed their sister, Ang Mei, as a figurehead monarch. Vietnamese officials ran the kingdom, Vietnamese people were encouraged to colonise Cambodia, and Vietnamese language and law, and even Vietnamese costumes and hairstyles, were increasingly insisted upon.

A country-wide rebellion broke out in 1840, and the Thais responded readily to calls for help from Ang Mei's brothers. For five nightmarish years Thai and Vietnamese forces, and also Cambodian factions, fought an inconclusive war, ravishing the countryside. Finally in 1845 the Thais and Vietnamese agreed to compromise, placing on the throne Ang Duang, son of Ang Chan, who would pay homage to both Bangkok and Hué. In this uneasy peace Ang Duang was encouraged by French missions (which had been operating in Cambodia since the previous century) to appeal for French support. In 1853 he sent feelers to the French diplomatic mission in Singapore, but King Mongkut of Thailand made clear his displeasure and the French backed off, for the time being.

The colonial era, 1863–1940

The French began their attack on Vietnam in 1859 and by 1862 had established the colony of Cochin China around Saigon. Cambodia, their new colony's hinterland, naturally interested them. They envisaged the Mekong as a mighty trade route, perhaps even offering access to China. At the same time a new Cambodian king, Norodom (reigned 1860–1904) was seeking allies to support him against the Thais and also domestic rivals for his throne.

In August 1863 he signed a treaty of 'protection' which established a French Resident at Phnom Penh, gave France control of Cambodia's foreign relations, and opened the country to French commercial interests. King Mongkut protested but in 1867 reluctantly recognised the French protectorate. The Thais retained Cambodia's northwestern provinces however. These would only be restored to Cambodia in 1907 at the insistence of the French.

For two decades the protectorate meant little change within Cambodia. The French soon realised that the country could offer no rapid economic return, and focussed their development energies on Cochin China. Equally, Norodom proved adept at turning aside French suggestions for administrative or social reform, as he would throughout his long reign.

In 1884 the French forced Norodom – under threat of being deposed and replaced – to sign an agreement intended to increase the number of French officials in the kingdom, give policy control to the French over all administrative, financial, judicial and commercial matters, initiate a land-titling system, and abolish slavery. The Cambodian ruling class was alarmed at its potential loss of power over taxation, trade, land and labour, and initiated a country-wide revolt. By 1886 the French were willing to acknowledge respect for Cambodian custom, and for another two decades change was minimal and cautiously introduced.

At Norodom's death in 1904, however, the French appointed from amongst the possible heirs a king willing to comply with French policies. He was the first of three kings chosen by the French on the basis of their apparent compliancy. The third would be Norodom Sihanouk, who ascended the throne as a shy nineteen year-old in 1941. From 1904, therefore, the French were able to establish complete authority over their protectorate. Prior to 1940 they encountered little further opposition. In 1925 the murder of a French official, Bardez, caused a sensation, but only because it seemed an isolated and uncharacteristic challenge to French rule.

Cambodia's economic resources proved to be scanty, even its human resources. In 1921 the population was assessed at about 2.5 million. The main crop was rice, and a Chinese-controlled rice export industry developed, purchasing rice from Khmer farmers, but Cambodian rice was generally considered to be inferior to and less efficiently produced than that of Cochin China. Small Chinese timber and pepper industries, and French-financed rubber estates using Vietnamese labour, added to Cambodia's limited exports. Other minor exports included maize, kapok, and dried fish from the Tonle Sap region. The French slowly developed road and rail communications – by 1941 a railway linked Phnom Penh and the Thai border – but the Mekong remained, as it had always been, Cambodia's main trade route. The port of Saigon dominated this riverine trade.

Around 95 per cent of Khmers remained subsistence farmers. They were characterised by the French – and also by the Chinese, Thais, Vietnamese and often their own elite – as 'lazy', 'ignorant', 'lacking initiative', 'fatalistic' and 'child-like'. Western observers dismissed them as a 'decadent race', compared with their ancestors of Angkor. The peasants' options were extremely limited however. French taxation levels were harsh. In addition there is evidence that the peasants' social superiors still extracted their traditional obligatory dues of product and labour, despite French abolition of formal slavery. In remoter regions endemic petty violence still made life insecure.

There were further factors deterring any change or development in peasant life. Cambodia was a country where commercial instincts had long been smothered by isolation, war and a ruling class which despised trade, other than as a source of taxation. Under French rule, Chinese and Vietnamese entrepreneurs quickly assumed dominance over trade and money-lending. In colonial Cambodia no industries of consequence were developed. The country's towns remained small (by the 1930s Phnom Penh's population was about 100,000, Battambang's 20,000) and dominated by aliens – French, Chinese and Vietnamese. Cambodia's elite acquired a French-language education from private tutors or abroad, but for the general population a meagre and essentially traditional education in Buddhist temple schools was all that was available. The first Khmer language newspaper only appeared in 1938.

Until the 1970s observers usually saw the lot of Cambodia's peasantry during the colonial era as a relatively happy one. The traumatic events in Cambodia since then have suggested that the countryside harboured much bitter frustration and resentment, waiting to be tapped.

World War II, 1940–1945

Such feelings were yet to be coherently expressed, much less given an outlet. In Cambodia politicisation really only began during World War II, and then it was cautious and involved limited numbers. By the 1940s a tiny Khmer intelligentsia had begun to form, focussed around three institutions – the scholarly Buddhist Institute, Cambodia's sole French-language high school in Phnom Penh, and the Khmer newspaper Nagara Vatta (Angkor Wat). Cambodian feelings were outraged in 1940 by the transfer back to Thailand, under Japanese auspices, of the northwestern provinces (these would be returned once more to Cambodia in 1947).

Nationalist stirrings could be tightly controlled by the French, however. The French reached an agreement with the Japanese which allowed them to continue to administer Indochina in exchange for the free movement of Japanese forces. Nagara Vatta was strictly censored, and suppressed in mid-1942 following a protest march in Phnom Penh by monks and nationalist-intellectuals over the arrest of a monk implicated in an anti-French plot. A key figure amongst the nationalists, Son Ngoc Thanh, escaped round-up at this point and went to Japan.

The French role in the evolution of Cambodian nationalism was mixed, however. Recognising the need to deflect popular fascination with Japanese power, the French launched a quasi-nationalist movement for young Cambodians, glorifying Cambodia's past and its future 'in partnership' with France. They also took steps to raise the status and salaries of Cambodians in government service. Unwittingly they fuelled developing nationalist feelings further by launching in 1943 a program to replace Cambodia's Indian-derived form of writing with a roman alphabet. (In Vietnam a comparable reform had been popularly accepted, in the interests of simplicity, efficiency and wider literacy.)

The Buddhist sangha and the intelligentsia rebelled against what they viewed as an attack on Cambodia's traditional learning and cultural heritage. The romanisation controversy kept up anti-French feeling until March 1945, when the Japanese seized control of government, interned the French and amongst other measures dropped the romanisation program.

In April 1945 the Japanese, now anxious to harness Cambodian nationalism for themselves, prodded a hesitant Norodom Sihanouk to declare Cambodia 'independent'. But when Japan surrendered to the Allies in August 1945 there was no coherent view amongst Cambodia's hereditary or intelligentsia elites about the next step for Cambodia. Cambodia still had no mass anti-colonial movement such as emerged in 1945 in Vietnam and Indonesia.

Towards independence, 1945–1953

After the Japanese surrender Cambodia drifted. French officials resumed authority and in October 1945 arrested Son Ngoc Thanh, who had returned to Cambodia in April and had become the main figure trying to organise resistance to the French return. At the same time the French opened discussions with King Sihanouk about limited Cambodian self-government. Faced with revolution in Vietnam, they recognised that some gesture towards Cambodia's aroused national feelings would be wise. They also needed the collaboration of Cambodia's elite to restore order in the countryside, where armed bands were flourishing. Some of these armed groups affected a degree of nationalism, calling themselves Khmer Issarak (Free Khmer). Both the strongly anti-French Thai government of the day and the Vietnamese communists were lending them tentative support.

The French, while retaining control of finance, defence, foreign affairs and all key instruments of government, announced elections for a new National Assembly and permitted political parties to form. At the elections, held in September 1946, the winning party proved to be the Democratic Party, which took 50 of the Assembly's 67 seats. The Democrats, though headed by a prince, broadly represented Cambodia's 'intelligentsia elite' – schoolteachers, minor government officials, politicised monks and the like – and convincingly demonstrated their ability to organise a strong grassroots vote. Cambodia's traditional royal and aristocratic ruling class, headed by the King, was not amused. Subsequent Democrat attempts to win meaningful powers for the National Assembly and achieve independence would be frustrated not only by the French but also by Sihanouk and those who supported the traditional social order.

By the early 1950s the lack of political progress was producing acute strains. The National Assembly had become a factionalised talk-shop. A radical fringe of politicised Cambodians were contemplating revolution, some under Son Ngoc

Thanh, who established an insurgent movement in the northwest in 1952, and some under the communist, Vietnamese sponsored, KPRP (Khmer People's Revolutionary Party, founded 1951), which was organising guerrilla activity in outlying areas. In January 1953 martial law was declared and Sihanouk dissolved the National Assembly.

Sihanouk now executed a dazzling bid for command of his people. Beginning in February 1953 he toured France, the United States and other countries demanding independence. In October 1953 the French – by this time with their backs to the wall in Vietnam – gave in to Sihanouk's campaign. Sihanouk returned to Cambodia a hero.

Cambodia under Sihanouk, 1953–1970

Independence defused most of the insurgency in the countryside. Son Ngoc Thanh dwindled into irrelevance in exile. The leaders of the KPRP retreated to Vietnam, though the party would continue surreptitious recruitment in Cambodia. In 1954 Sihanouk and the conservative elite regarded the Democratic Party as their main challenge, especially as they were obliged to hold national elections in September 1955 under agreements reached at the international Geneva Conference on Indochina in 1954.

Sihanouk responded to this challenge with more strategic brilliance. In March 1955 he abdicated (his father became a figurehead king but would die in 1960) and established his own political party, Sangkum Reastr Niyum (People's Socialist Community). His new-found, if vague, commitment to socialism was perhaps designed to distance himself from his conservative background and woo the leftist-inclined intelligentsia. In the same vein he announced that Cambodia would be unaligned with either the communist or anti-communist world blocs, though he continued to accept the United States' military and economic aid to Cambodia which had begun under the French.

Simultaneously Democrat supporters found themselves facing violent intimidation from Sihanouk's security forces. Voting procedures at the elections were flagrantly fixed. It is debatable who would have won free and fair elections – Sihanouk the national hero and now apparently a political progressive, or the Democrats – but in the event Sihanouk's Sangkum won every seat in the Assembly. After continuing harassment the Democratic Party dissolved in 1957. Sihanouk, though technically no longer king, now truly seemed to be monarch of all he surveyed.

For over a decade after 1955 he continued to show great adroitness and energy. He personally oversaw all facets of government, controlled news and information, and regularly addressed the people. His rhetoric of 'Buddhist Socialism', coming from the lips of a man who retained the aura of a semi-divine king, seemed to offer something for everyone. He bemused his critics of both the left and the right, leaving them unsure where he, or they, stood. Sihanouk enjoyed surprising people with sudden switches of policy, though whether these switches arose from calculation or whim was never clear. The sole constant of his rule was intolerance of opposition. Hundreds of dissidents 'disappeared' during this period. Stifling the discord which undoubtedly would have appeared in a more open political system was Sihanouk's main, if dubious, domestic achievement. He gave Cambodia a kind of peace, which in later years many Cambodians would fondly remember. Another domestic achievement was the expansion of education, on which Sihanouk spent as much as 20 per cent of the national budget. Large numbers of secondary and tertiary educated young people emerged. Crucially, however, Sihanouk was uninterested in economic matters, and under him the Cambodian economy, after initial growth, went into decline. The combination of stifled political life, an expanding educated class (many of whom were unemployed or underemployed) and a decaying economy would prove disastrous for Sihanouk and Cambodia's domestic peace.

Looming over that peace was the resumed conflict in neighbouring Vietnam. Sihanouk was anxious to save his country from involvement in the conflict, but he also wanted to position Cambodia and himself to be on good terms with the victor. To these ends he proclaimed Cambodia's neutrality but judged it expedient to tilt to the left in foreign and domestic policy. In 1963 he rejected United States aid and nationalised Cambodia's banks and import-export trade in the name of 'socialism'. In 1965 he broke off diplomatic relations with the United States. Secretly, meanwhile, he accepted the use of Cambodian territory by North Vietnamese forces and the southern Vietnamese NLF insurgents in their fight against the United States-backed Saigon regime. Openly he established cordial relations with China, perhaps hoping that China might restrain any larger Vietnamese designs on Cambodia.

The rejection of United States aid reduced Cambodia's income significantly and disgruntled Cambodia's conservatives, particularly in the military. Nationalisation disgruntled the business elite, heightened inefficiency and corruption, and led to hard times for the people. Sihanouk's toleration of Vietnamese (who received supplies via the Cambodian port of Sihanoukville) forces on Cambodian soil disturbed patriotic Cambodian sentiment.

Around 1966 Sihanouk seems to have tired of his political juggling. His 'hands-on' control diminished and the power of the conservative forces in Sangkum and his administration increased. Popularly there was growing disillusionment with Sihanouk's policies and style, at least in urban areas. The countryside presented a mixed picture; Sihanouk's prestige remained high with many rural people, but in remoter areas a small but revivified communist insurgency was gaining ground. In 1967–68 government forces brutally crushed a peasant revolt in the north-west to which the communists had given leadership. (The revolt was caused by government seizures of rice at low prices under

Sihanouk's nationalisation policies.) In 1969 Sihanouk cautiously re-opened diplomatic relations with the United States, but this now seemed more a sign of indecisiveness than of his old political skills. In March 1970, while Sihanouk was overseas, the predominantly conservative National Assembly withdrew confidence in Sihanouk as head of state. The principal force behind the move was Sihanouk's cousin and deputy prime minister Sisowath Sirik Matak. Sihanouk's prime minister and long-time associate Lon Nol went along with the move, and became head of the new government of the 'Khmer Republic' declared in October 1970.

War and revolution, 1970–1975

The coup against Sihanouk polarised the population. The Lon Nol government initially enjoyed significant support, but Sihanouk rallied anti-government opinion. In late March 1970 he broadcast from Beijing, appealing to people to 'engage in guerrilla warfare in the jungles against our enemies'. The main beneficiaries of his appeal were the communist insurgents, who now enjoyed Sihanouk's blessing and prestige. Moving swiftly to capitalise on their windfall, the communists effectively ranged the countryside against Phnom Penh and other urban areas by 1972. Meanwhile the Lon Nol government proved tragically inept. A series of drives by government forces against the Vietnamese forces in Cambodia in 1970–71 were repulsed with massive casualties, permanently weakening the government's military capabilities. Ironically, the Vietnamese would withdraw from Cambodia voluntarily in early 1973.

The United States backed the Lon Nol government, but resumed United States aid which served mainly to foster gross corruption in the administration and the military. Lon Nol suffered a stroke in 1971 and failed thereafter to give strong leadership to his factionalised and increasingly demoralised power base. United States bombing of the countryside – massive in intensity and appallingly destructive – probably slowed the communist-led advance on Phnom Penh but also drove many of the population to support the insurgency and to regard the United States-aligned urban areas with bitter hatred.

In the United States, dwindling confidence in President Nixon and growing opposition to his handling of the Indochina conflict led the United States Congress to end the bombing of Cambodia. Thereafter it was a matter of time before the Lon Nol regime collapsed. The insurgents took Phnom Penh on 17th April 1975.

'Democratic Kampuchea': Khmer Rouge government 1975–1979

The name 'Khmer Rouge' (strictly 'Khmers Rouges' – red Khmers) was popularised by Sihanouk in the 1960s as a term for leftist anti-government forces in the countryside. It has remained the name in general use for the forces who took power in 1975, set up a state they called 'Democratic Kampuchea', and who, after their overthrow in 1979, resumed rural-based insurgency. In April 1975, however, these forces called themselves *'angkar padevat'* (revolutionary organisation). Their communist leadership was not made explicit until September 1977 when the existence of the CPK (Communist Party of Kampuchea) was announced.

The CPK had been set up in 1968, to resume the insurgency tactics abandoned by the former Khmer People's Revolutionary Party (KPRP) in 1954. In the intervening years the KPRP, based in Vietnam, had continued underground recruitment in Cambodia. Its most famous recruit in retrospect was a young middle-class, Paris-educated schoolteacher, Saloth Sar, who would take the name Pol Pot and rise to leadership of the CPK.

Under Pol Pot the CPK devised a ferociously radical program of reform for Cambodia. In April 1975 the country was sealed off from the outside world. Phnom Penh and other urban centres were forcefully evacuated and left mostly to decay. All Cambodians were to become farmers under the direction of angkar. Markets, private trade and the use of money were abolished. Professional activity ceased. Books were forbidden and education was abandoned except for propaganda sessions. Religion was proscribed and the *sangha* (order of monks) dispersed; many former places of worship were levelled. Angkar dictated peoples' movements, activities, food allowances and dress. Former upper and middle class people, former government employees, most professionals and most educated people were treated as expendable labour in the countryside. Many died.

Pol Pot's government glorified ancient Angkor but otherwise almost wholly repudiated Cambodia's past. A totally new 'Kampuchea' was going to be built, starting in 1975 – 'year zero'. The origins of this apocalyptic program have been much debated by commentators. Influences on the CPK leadership may have included extreme left-wing theories fashionable in France in the 1950s and 1960s and Mao's 'great leap forward' and 'cultural revolution' in China. But 'Pol Potism' was distinctively Cambodian in making popular resentment of Cambodia's humiliating national history the main driving force of revolution. The revolution's enemies were not only the class enemies defined by Marx but any foreign peoples who had degraded Cambodia – led by the Vietnamese, Thais and Americans – and any Cambodians who had colluded with them, which to the CPK meant all city folk. The brutal simplicity of these doctrines, and the vision of building a new Khmer society, untainted by foreigners and the old elite, appealed particularly to youth. The lower echelons of angkar were mainly made up of young people, many still teenagers.

The consequences of the CPK's program were catastrophic. Conditions of life varied from province to province, but hardship was severe to extreme everywhere. While an estimated 500,000 Cambodians had died during the 1970 – 75 war, over one million more would die under Khmer Rouge rule, from brutality and callousness, mismanagement, malnutrition, disease and the virtual abolition of medical services.

The CPK leadership's particular hatred of the Vietnamese had several consequences. Firstly, the party began to repudiate its Vietnamese-sponsored background. The repudiation turned into a purge of CPK cadres and members who had been trained in Vietnam or who were thought to sympathise with Vietnam's communist government. Tens of thousands died, often after brutal torture, though some escaped to Vietnam. Secondly, Cambodian forces staged repeated incursions into Vietnam, seeking re-definition of the Viet–Cambodian border. Thirdly, Viet–Cambodian relations came to mirror the great split in the communist world – while Vietnam was closely aligned with the USSR, Cambodia moved under the protection of China. Vietnam staged a warning offensive into Cambodia in late 1977, but subsequently withdrew its troops, massing them along the border. Provocation continued, however, and on Christmas Day 1978 the Vietnamese again invaded. Khmer Rouge forces collapsed before them and the Vietnamese entered a ghostly Phnom Penh on the 7th of January 1979. Soon Vietnamese forces in Cambodia would number 250,000. They failed, however, to capture Pol Pot or his close colleagues.

Cambodia as a 'Vietnamese protectorate', 1979–1991

Though initially welcomed by most Cambodians, the Vietnamese were aware of the centuries-old fear of Vietnam in the country. They also knew that their invasion of a sovereign nation, however repellent its government, could bring international condemnation. Thus they rapidly established the People's Republic of Kampuchea (PRK) under a government headed by Cambodians, mostly former CPK members who had fled the party's purges. These included Heng Samrin, head of state, and Hun Sen, who would become premier in 1985. Although another one-party state, the new government was relatively laissez faire in the economic and social fields, dismantling the Khmer Rouge's collective farming and restoring the use of money and private trade.

However Cambodian society was by now utterly destabilised. Before traditional farming could be restored Cambodia suffered terrible famine. Only by the mid-1980s would the traditional subsistence economy regain equilibrium and the shops and markets of the towns return to precarious life. Meanwhile the PRK, like Vietnam, became an international pariah, supported only by the Soviet bloc and some neutral nations such as India. The United States, China, Thailand and the other ASEAN nations led international condemnation of the Vietnamese presence in Cambodia and of the PRK 'puppet' government. Denied legitimacy the PRK was also denied much international economic aid and trade.

The pawns in this stand-off, apart from the general Cambodian population, were hundreds of thousands of Cambodian refugees camped along the Thai–Cambodian border, who had fled variously war, famine, the Khmer Rouge or the Vietnamese occupation. Working amongst them were two Cambodian political organisations – the Khmer Rouge, and the KPNLF (Khmer People's National Liberation Front), a non-communist, anti-Vietnamese body headed by Son Sann, a former prime minister. The Khmer Rouge enjoyed the staunch backing of China, then also at loggerheads with Vietnam, and received Chinese military aid funnelled through Thailand. Despite its grotesque record the Khmer Rouge also enjoyed international prestige as Cambodia's 'legitimate' government, holding Cambodia's seat at the United Nations. Inside Cambodia the Khmer Rouge maintained a shadowy guerrilla presence, despite every effort by Vietnamese and PRK forces to eliminate it.

In the early 1980s Sihanouk and his son Prince Norodom Ranariddh also established an anti-PRK organisation, FUNCINPEC (French acronym for National United Front for an Independent, Neutral, Peaceful and Co-operative Cambodia). Sihanouk had survived the years of Khmer Rouge government under virtual house arrest (he lost 14 children and grandchildren in those years) and was now based in Beijing or sometimes North Korea. In mid-1982 a shaky coalition was carpentered between the three Cambodian anti-PRK organisations. The Khmer Rouge announced the abolition of the CPK and claimed to be abandoning its former policies. Few believed this.

The international impasse continued through the 1980s. In 1989 Vietnam withdrew its troops from Cambodia, partly because the PRK government now appeared self-sustaining but mainly because of Vietnam's loss of Soviet aid following the collapse of the USSR. In Cambodia the PRK transformed itself in 1990 into the SOC (State of Cambodia) which effectively committed itself to a private enterprise economy, as Vietnam and China were doing. The SOC government also became active in restoring Cambodian Buddhism.

The ending of the Cold War and the changing economic goals of China and Vietnam opened the possibility of ending the stand-off over Cambodia. After much diplomacy in which Australia and Indonesia played a key role, twenty nations convened in Paris in October 1991. The conference persuaded the SOC government and the three opposition organisations to form a coalition administration pending national elections under United Nations supervision. The inclusion of the Khmer Rouge in this arrangement shocked many people, inside and outside Cambodia, but the move has been defended as the only means of breaking the deadlock, given China's inability to abandon the Khmer Rouge without losing international face. The assumption of responsibility for Cambodia by the U.N. and the promised elections – which the Khmer Rouge would be unlikely to win – gave China the chance to discard its by now embarrassing ties with the Khmer Rouge.

UNTAC, the 1993 elections and the Royal Government of Cambodia

The United Nations established UNTAC (United Nations Transitional Authority in Cambodia) which came to consist of 22,000 personnel, two thirds of them military, from a number of nations. UNTAC's main tasks were to disarm the forces of all four Cambodian factions, repatriate the refugees, monitor the coalition administration of the country (in practice the SOC administration and security apparatus retained great power) and prepare the planned elections. UNTAC's achievements were mixed.

The refugees were repatriated but the disarmament process collapsed in May 1992 when the Khmer Rouge, and then SOC, refused to participate. UNTAC also failed to deal with charges that the SOC security forces were using violence against their coalition partners, especially Sihanouk's FUNCINPEC. Sihanouk himself played an unnerving role in this period, appearing in Cambodia to warm popular acclaim but disappearing back to Beijing or Pyongyang with expressions of displeasure and foreboding.

UNTAC won plaudits, however, for its handling of the elections in May 1993. Nearly 90 per cent of enrolled voters (close to 5 million) went to the polls, despite threats of Khmer Rouge violence. The Khmer Rouge had decided to boycott the elections, presumably fearing a dismal rebuff from the people. FUNCINPEC candidates won 58 of the available 120 assembly seats. Candidates from the former SOC government contested the election as the CPP (Cambodian Peoples Party) and won 51 seats. Son Sann's group, now the BLDP (Buddhist Liberal Democratic Party), took 10 seats, and a minor party the one remaining seat.

Elements of the CPP disputed these results but others manoeuvred to retain a prominent role in government – a role they were virtually guaranteed anyway, given CPP strength in the bureaucracy, military and police. The following months of deal-making seemed to many observers to decline into a scramble by all parties for the perks of office, a scramble complicated by factionalism within each of the parties.

Two months after the election an interim coalition administration was formed, which in September became the Royal Government of Cambodia – in the same month the Assembly recognised Sihanouk as Cambodia's King once more. Heading the coalition government were Prince Norodom Ranariddh (FUNCINPEC) as 'first' prime minister and Hun Sen (CPP) as 'second' prime minister. Similar balances had been constructed throughout the various ministries. King Sihanouk – technically now a constitutional monarch presiding over a pluralistic, democratic political system – continued to intervene in policy-making, despite reports that he was now ill with cancer. Some saw his actions as destabilising meddling, others as constructive attempts to balance the antagonistic forces grouped within the government.

Cambodia in the mid 1990s

The coalition government, at present 50 per cent financed by foreign aid, has proved much weaker than hoped for. Little progress has been made in strengthening Cambodia's shattered economy and infrastructure or in building urgently needed social services. International aid projects and foreign and domestic private enterprise have been encouraged by the 'technocrats' who hold the economic portfolios, but face an otherwise irresolute government, a still inadequate legal framework, and an undisciplined and corrupted bureaucracy, customs service, police force and military.

The weakness of the government arises partly from its calamitous inheritance. It also arises from internal rivalries. These include strained relations between First Prime Minister Ranariddh and Sihanouk's half-brother and Foreign Minister Prince Norodom Sirivudh. Second Prime Minister and CPP leader Hun Sen appears to be struggling for control of his party with Sar Kheng, Deputy Prime Minister and Joint Interior Minister. The rivalries and ambitions of other figures are an ongoing source of gossip in Phnom Penh. In July 1994 the government aborted an attempted coup led, supposedly, by Prince Norodom Chakrapong (Ranariddh's half-brother) and Sin Song, both of the CPP, though Hun Sen repudiated wider CPP involvement in the affair. Popularly, respect for the government, the Assembly and the parties has plummeted.

The Khmer Rouge, meanwhile, has strengthened its presence in provincial areas, particularly in the northwest and southwest. During fighting in the 1994 dry season (February to May) Khmer Rouge forces humiliated government troops in the northwest. Khmer Rouge forces are variously estimated to number from 5,000 to 20,000. The government claims that they are still receiving military aid from elements of the Thai military, a claim denied by the Thai government.

The strategy of the Khmer Rouge leadership appears to be to broaden their forces' grip in the countryside and undermine confidence in the government, at home and abroad, while waiting for the government to self-destruct. The future of the Khmer Rouge does not appear assured, however. Its leadership is ageing, and in a virtually post-communist world they do not have the degree of outside support they once enjoyed. Their level of control over the scattered units calling themselves Khmer Rouge is uncertain.

Cambodian government forces are supposed to number 140,000, but up to half of these may be 'ghost soldiers' – non-existent troops whose pay and supplies are expropriated by the officer corps. Officers also misappropriate the pay and supplies (including arms and ammunition) of actual troops. Morale and discipline are generally poor. The international community is reluctant to grant additional resources to such a corrupted organisation.

The above uncertainties, combined with King Sihanouk being in the twilight of his years of influence and without an agreed successor, are extremely worrying. History has shown that Cambodia's fortunes rise and fall depending upon the policies of its larger and more powerful neighbours. Current events suggest little has changed.

TIMELINES

late 1980s: Non-oil exports exceed oil exports and Indonesian economy undergoes steady liberalisation and internationalisation

1965: New Order government under President Suharto

1965: Unsuccessful coup attempt by some army officers

1959-65: Period of Guided Democracy

1950: President Sukarno elected leader of independent Indonesia

1946-49: Dutch resume control and guerrilla war starts

1945: Independence unilaterally declared on 17 August

1942-45: Japanese occupation

1796: VOC bankrupt and control assumed by the Dutch government

1602: Netherlands East India Company (VOC) formed and attacks Jayakarta in 1619

16th century: Portuguese first to establish trading posts

13th century: Islam spreads throughout archipelago

6th-8th centuries: Borobudur and Prambanan temples built

Indonesia

Indonesia's geography is an integral part of its history. A sprawling archipelago straddling the equator, Indonesia has more than 13,500 islands, ranging from tiny areas that not so long ago were merely atolls to the huge island of Sumatra. In the mid 1990s it has over 185 million people, spread very unevenly across these islands. At one extreme, about 100 million live on densely populated Java; at the other the large resource-rich island of Kalimantan is sparsely populated. Indonesia is a tropical country with a volcanic spine running through its islands. Many volcanos are still active, every so often wreaking destruction on surrounding peoples and crops. But the volcanic soil and the tropical climate have made most of Indonesia extremely fertile, nowhere more so than the river valleys of Java where prosperous kingdoms have waxed and waned over more than a thousand years.

The Indonesian coat of arms bears the inscription 'Unity in Diversity'. The diversity of Indonesia is apparent to even the most casual observer. There are over 300 socio-linguistic groups in Indonesia, each with a distinct culture and heritage. Only about one in six Indonesians speaks the national language at home. Even fewer speak Indonesian as their first language. The mother tongue of the vast majority is a regional language, for example, Javanese, Balinese, Minangkabau or Acehnese. Nursery rhymes, childhood stories, myths, legends and cultural mores are as diverse as the languages. Not surprisingly, most Indonesians first develop a regional identity, only learning the national language, Indonesian, when they begin school and with it an Indonesian identity.

In the major cities of Jakarta, Surabaya, Bandung and Medan there are significant numbers of people who speak Indonesian in the home and identify themselves as Indonesians from childhood. The diversity of Indonesia is an enormous challenge to the modern State. Nation building in Indonesia is no mere slogan, nor is it merely a euphemism for economic development. The Indonesian government is acutely aware that national unity and a national cultural identity have to be created. The regional identity that most Indonesians acquire automatically, together with the country's cultural and linguistic diversity, makes nation building and the development of social cohesiveness a long–term and difficult task.

Pre-colonial Indonesia

Southeast Asia lies astride the great trading routes from China to India. For over two thousand years there are records of traders sailing their ships between China and Southeast Asia and between Southeast Asia and India. Southeast Asia, and especially the Indonesian archipelago, was a source of spices, gourmet foods, sandalwood, medicines and other tropical products. Chinese, Arabic and Indian traders were a common sight in the ports which dotted the area.

There were two broad types of states in the Indonesian archipelago in the pre-modern period. First were the coastal states. Located at the mouths of rivers with good secure harbours, they were dependent on regional and international trade. The most prominent of these were on, or close to, the Straits of Malaka through which shipping between China and India (and later Europe and China) had to pass – on the east and south coast of Sumatra and on the north Java coast. Second were the inland states. The wealth of these states was based on rich agricultural production from the volcanic soils of the alluvial plains. The most prominent of these were in Central and East Java and in Bali.

The earliest kingdoms in the Indonesian archipelago were Hindu/Buddhist states. Hinduism and Buddhism came to Southeast Asia from India, spreading along the trade routes and adopted by local rulers attracted by the Court ritual and religious/philosophical ideas. Today visitors to Indonesia flock to the central Javanese city of Yogyakarta. Together with its neighbouring city of Solo, Yogyakarta is the heartland of the Javanese, the centre of their history, culture and philosophy. Within thirty kilometres of Yogyakarta are two great religious monuments, the Buddhist temple of Borobudur and the Hindu temple of Prambanan. Both were built out of local stone between the 6th and the 8th centuries, hundreds of years before the medieval cathedrals of Europe were begun. Restoration projects have revealed the stunning beauty of the temples, their sheer scale of construction and the intricately carved bas reliefs which adorn them from top to bottom. These are religious monuments, dating from a time when Hinduism and Buddhism were the predominant religions in Java. They are evidence of the prosperity of the kingdoms to which they belonged, the engineering knowledge of their people, their craftsmanship and their artistry. Borobudur and Prambanan temples are the finest in Indonesia, but hundreds of other smaller temples can be found throughout Java. The Balinese remain predominantly Hindu and there are many thousands of old and new temples on Bali.

Muslim traders are recorded in the Indonesian archipelago as early as the 6th century, but the Islamisation of Indonesia began in the 13th century with the conversion of the ruler of Aceh, at the northern tip of Sumatra. We know little about this but it is clear that the process of Islamisation of Indonesia was very slow, with people absorbing Islamic beliefs into existing religious and philosophical systems as they adapted Islam to Indonesian soil. When the Dutch arrived in Indonesia at the beginning of the 17th century the kingdoms they engaged with were almost all Islamic, with Hinduism restricted to Bali. But the nature of Indonesian Islam varied greatly, and still does in the 1990s. There is a broad spectrum of practices and intensities of belief, ranging from the Acehnese, who are generally more publicly Islamic and more strict adherents to the principles of the Koran than others in Indonesia, to the people of central and east Java who have a more relaxed Islamic faith sustained alongside pre-Islamic beliefs and practices.

The inland kingdoms were prosperous agrarian states generating considerable agricultural surpluses. They were strongly hierarchical states with taxation systems extracting agricultural products and labour from the peasants. They developed legal systems and bureaucratic structures. The agricultural surpluses supported large courts and the skilled workers needed to build the massive stone temples. The courts promoted high cultures of music, dance and literature. The great Indian epic poems, the Mahabharata and the Ramayana were adapted by court musicians, dancers and master puppeteers as vehicles for the transmission of Javanese or Balinese ethics and cultural values. Writing systems were based on Sanskrit with many Sanskrit words entering local languages.

When the Europeans arrived in Southeast Asia in the middle of the 16th century there were well established States across the whole of Southeast Asia. The early European visitors marvelled at the prosperity of Southeast Asia, the health of its peoples and the sophistication of its high cultures. There were long-standing trading networks linking the Southeast Asian states and a tradition of shipbuilding and maritime skills which saw traders from Southeast Asia ply their wares as far afield as China and India. The major Indonesian states were at Aceh, on the northern tip of Sumatra, in Central Java, in Bali, in the Malukas and Sulawesi and on the north coast of Java. They competed vigorously, sometimes waging war on each other. There was a constant flow of goods and peoples across the archipelago using Malay as the medium of communication.

Colonialism

The Portuguese were the first Europeans to acquire outposts in Asia. In the 16th century they established trading posts and colonial outposts in places as disparate as Goa in India, Malaka in Malaysia, Ambon and Timor in Indonesia and Macau in China. By the beginning of the seventeenth century the power of catholic Portugal and Spain was waning in the face of the emerging protestant nations of England and the Netherlands. The English East India Company and the Netherlands United East India Company (VOC) were established in 1600 and 1602 respectively. For nearly two hundred years they were fierce commercial rivals in Asia. The VOC moved quickly to establish trading posts in India, Ceylon, Taiwan and China seeking the produce of 'the Orient'. A major target was the spice islands, in what are now Sulawesi and Maluku in eastern Indonesia. The VOC first became involved in the Indonesian archipelago through trading with local kingdoms, but its desire to monopolise the spice trade to Europe quickly caused it to eject the Portuguese from Ambon in Maluku and then to destroy the local kingdoms. In 1619 the VOC launched an attack on Jayakarta, then a major fort and trading town of the West Java kingdom of Banten where the VOC had been peacefully trading for a number of years. The Bantenese were driven out and on the ashes of the razed town the VOC established its headquarters for the archipelago. Jayakarta was re-named Batavia, a name which was retained for the capital of the Netherlands East Indies until the declaration of independence in August 1945 when it was again re-named, this time as Jakarta.

The VOC slowly extended its physical presence in the Indonesian archipelago. Throughout the 17th and 18th centuries it behaved much like a local kingdom, creating and breaking alliances with rival kingdoms to make war on its enemies and trading widely both within the archipelago and with China, India and Europe. But there were crucial differences which eventually enabled the Dutch to conquer the archipelago. First, the VOC had a power base outside the archipelago with gunboats and troops stationed throughout Asia able to be brought into battle against indigenous rulers. Second, the VOC had a broader strategic framework, and against traditional ruling elites with little experience of the world outside the archipelago they were able to take advantage of the rivalry between local kingdoms. Third, by the 18th century they had superior weaponry.

Nevertheless, it was not until 1756 that the VOC controlled the whole of Java, when it divided the Mataram Court of Central Java against itself. The VOC went bankrupt in 1796, wracked by corruption. It then controlled Java, Ambon and small nearby islands and small enclaves in central and southern Sumatra. It was the biggest, most powerful State in the archipelago, but most of what is now Indonesia still lay outside its control. The Netherlands Crown took over the assets of the VOC and, after a brief interlude of British control of Java during the Napoleonic Wars, the East Indies reverted to Dutch rule. Gradually, through the nineteenth century the Netherlands East Indies Government extended its control over Sumatra and eastern Indonesia. With the destruction of the Balinese kingdoms in 1905 and the defeat of the powerful kingdom of Aceh in 1911 the colony was complete. The Dutch often talked of their three hundred years in the Netherlands East Indies, but for most people in the archipelago incorporation into the Netherlands East Indies occurred towards the end of the nineteenth century or in the first decade of the twentieth century. Local pride, regional political, cultural and personal loyalties and a sense of local history remained strong when the Japanese destroyed the Dutch empire in 1941.

By the beginning of the twentieth century the Dutch had created the Netherlands East Indies as a centralised state, with power concentrated in the capital Batavia (now Jakarta), an efficient bureaucracy and a police and military service able to maintain social control. After the bitter experience of fighting the fiercely Islamic kingdom of Aceh for over 40 years the colonial government maintained a careful watch on Islamic religious leaders. Its policy distinguished between Islam as a religion and Islam as a political force. Religious observance was interfered with as little as possible, though mosques, Islamic schools and religious teachers were carefully monitored to ensure that they did nothing to rally people against the colonial state. Islamic leaders' involvement in political activities was not only carefully monitored but was ruthlessly quashed if they appeared to be gathering local support. The Dutch promoted a western educated secular elite built on the children of the pre-colonial elites and made every effort to prevent the development of a modernised Islamic elite.

The Dutch economic impact on the Indonesian archipelago was enormous. In their successful efforts to control the quantity and prices of the products of the archipelago they gradually destroyed regional trading networks that had existed for hundreds of years, serviced in large part by indigenous traders who plied the area and sailed as far as India to the west and China to the north. Indigenous traders were henceforth restricted to local trade. External trade became the exclusive preserve of European companies and inter-regional trade the preserve of Chinese who were encouraged to immigrate from southern China.

Javanese agriculture in particular was transformed by the Dutch in the 19th century. They created what they called a 'Cultivation System', by which Javanese farmers were compelled to produce designated crops for sale to the State at fixed prices. The crops – sugar, indigo, coffee and tea in the main – were then processed and transported for sale to European markets. By the end of the 19th century Java was the world's largest sugar producer. Sugar mills were built throughout rural Java to process the raw cane and railways and ports constructed to take the export crops to market. Village Java, largely a subsistence economy before 1830, was transformed. The subsistence economy gave way to a much more diversified economy, the population steadily grew until by the end of the 19th century there was little uncultivated land left and towns and cities sprang up to service the burgeoning export trade. By the beginning of the 20th century most Javanese no longer owned land, working as tenant farmers, share croppers or wage labourers in the local area and nearby towns.

The economic transformation of Sumatra in the first thirty years of the 20th century was equally dramatic. Huge areas of virgin forest made way for tobacco and rubber plantations. Sumatra became one of the world's largest and finest suppliers of tobacco and together with Malaya its largest supplier of rubber. When oil was discovered in the 1920s it became the springboard for what was to become the Royal Dutch Shell Oil Company.

Much of the labour which opened up Sumatra was Chinese. Chinese had long been resident in the Indonesian archipelago, predominantly as traders and merchants, and there had been a steady growth in their numbers in the 17th and 18th centuries. The great expansion, however, was part of the wider process of Chinese migration to Southeast Asia, Australia, the Pacific and the United States after the acquisition of Hong Kong by Britain in 1842 and the forced opening of Treaty ports on the south China coast. In the Netherlands East Indies they became not only traders, shopkeepers and urban workers but labourers on plantations, in tin and coal mines and on wharves and ships. They were never a large proportion of the colony's population, less than three per cent, but by the 20th century were dominant in local trade and urban commerce.

The economic transformation of Indonesia led to an accelerating process of urbanisation. By the mid 1910s the major cities on Java were already unable to cope with the migration from rural areas. The increasingly densely populated poorer parts of the towns and cities had low quality houses, with no sanitation systems or piped water. They flooded badly during the annual monsoon season and their peoples were wracked by malaria and water borne diseases such as cholera and typhoid. The colonial government lacked the political will to tackle these urban problems. By the 1920s the problems were probably beyond its capacity to solve. Living conditions for most urban Indonesians steadily worsened from the 1920s through to the 1970s.

The Dutch introduced western education in order to provide the skilled labour needed by the expanding colonial economy. The best schools used Dutch as the medium of instruction, graduation from which led to the better paid administrative jobs or the possibility of entering a University in the Netherlands or the medical and law schools in the colony. But entry to these schools for Indonesians was very difficult and, those few on scholarships aside, in practice was restricted to children of the indigenous elites or government officials. It was easier to get a modicum of education in schools where the medium of instruction was the vernacular language. Even so, at the end of the Dutch colonial era the literacy rate in Indonesia was lower than in that of any other European colony in Asia, with the exception of the Portuguese colony of East Timor.

Nationalism

The first people to regard themselves as Indonesian rather than Javanese, Acehnese or a member of one of the other ethnic groups, were young men and women who had received a western education at local high schools and subsequently at universities in the Netherlands. The term 'Indonesia' was first used in the early 1920s, but by 1928 the idea of being Indonesian and the determination to create a modern Indonesian nation free from Dutch colonial rule was widely held. In 1928 a national Youth Congress was held in Batavia at which thousands of emotionally aroused youths witnessed the ceremonial raising of the red and white flag, recited a National Pledge and sang a newly composed national song. This was a public expression of their determination to create an independent Indonesia with a common flag, language (Indonesian, which was derived from Malay) and national identity which transcended regional and ethnic loyalties.

The first stirrings of nationalism in the 1910s were seen by the Dutch colonial government as potentially dangerous but not an immediate threat. As political parties enrolled thousands of members and as newspapers and propaganda handbills were widely distributed the colonial laws were made more restrictive and political activists repeatedly jailed or exiled from the colony. The Dutch could never understand the intensity of nationalist feelings and had no plans for the colony's political development beyond vague references to the possibility of self-government eventually.

The Indonesian Communist Party (PKI) tried a revolutionary path to independence in a badly planned uprising in November 1926 and January 1927. The only result was that thousands of Indonesians, many of whom had only a marginal connection with the PKI, were either jailed or exiled to a political prison on the malaria infested upper reaches of the Digul River in what is now West Irian. There they stayed until brought to Australian jails in 1942 in the wake of the Japanese occupation of Indonesia. Ironically, they did not long remain in jail once Australian trade unionists realised that they were political prisoners. Many of them became leaders of a campaign to support Indonesian Independence in 1945 and 1946. This resulted in Australian trade union black bans on Dutch shipping and the Australian government's diplomatic support of the Indonesian Republic against the Dutch.

The most prominent Indonesian nationalist from the mid 1920s was a young engineering graduate named Sukarno. Before he was exiled in February 1934, Sukarno laid the basis for his dominant political position after 1945 as President of Indonesia. Sukarno alternately charmed and irritated his fellow nationalists, but even his strongest opponents admired the brilliance of his oratory. Wherever he went he drew large and enthusiastic crowds to his political rallies in both large cities and small towns.

More than any other person Sukarno succeeded in spreading the simple message of freedom to a wider cross section of urban and rural Indonesians than ever before. He popularised the nationalist ideology – the simple idea that his people were Indonesians and must set aside their religious and ethnic differences to unite in opposition to colonial rule. Although he was exiled in 1934 his memory lingered on in the minds of ordinary Indonesians who had heard him speak or been charmed by his charismatic personality or had simply heard of his heroic qualities from others.

Two issues were not resolved by the colonial nationalist movement, both of which became major issues in Indonesian politics in the 1950s and 1960s. Firstly, was the question of the role of Islam in Indonesia. The mainstream of the nationalist movement in the 1920s and 1930s was in agreement that an independent Indonesia should be a secular state. This position was adopted partly because of the religious diversity of Indonesia where although Muslims were in an overwhelming majority only a minority of these were strict adherents to Islamic teachings and precepts. A secular state was seen as a way of avoiding conflict. Some Islamic political parties disagreed and after independence strengthened their demands for national laws to be based on Islamic teaching. In contemporary Indonesia this is still one of the most sensitive issues.

A second major unresolved issue was whether Indonesia needed a social and economic revolution, or whether political independence was a sufficient goal. The advocates of major social and economic reforms were in a minority in the 1920s and 1930s. The dominant view was that Indonesians should concentrate on achieving independence and concern themselves about these potentially divisive issues after this was achieved. Those who wanted more fundamental social and economic reforms revived their activities in the 1950s. Their criticism was then directed at an Indonesian government in the hands of those who had led the nationalist movement since the late 1920s.

The Japanese Occupation

The Japanese occupied Indonesia in March 1942. There was little resistance from the Dutch. Initially they were welcomed by many Indonesians, glad to be freed from Dutch rule and impressed by Japanese propaganda slogans such as 'Japan the Light of Asia' and the 'East Asian Co-Prosperity Sphere'. However, it did not take very long for the Japanese to alienate themselves from all levels of Indonesian society. The romusha program on Java, whereby all able bodied males were required to provide free labour for the war effort, affected almost every family. Most romusha labour was used within the colony, on projects such as building railway lines and ships and on infrastructure construction. But hundreds of thousands were sent overseas to work on the construction of the Thai–Burma railway and Japanese projects elsewhere in Southeast Asia. Rice production on Java fell, through Japanese mismanagement as much as any other cause, and food and clothing were soon in desperately short supply. Indonesians quickly learnt that despite Japanese propaganda stressing Asian solidarity against Europeans, they were treated as distinctly inferior people by the Japanese.

However, Japanese occupation policies had some long term benefits for Indonesia. First, in removing the Dutch from administrative functions the Japanese elevated Indonesians to positions they would not have been able to obtain under colonial rule. This administrative experience proved useful after 1945. Second, they prohibited the use of the Dutch language and, while promoting Japanese, were pragmatic enough to realise that few Indonesians would be able to master that language quickly. They therefore also encouraged the use of Indonesian, in schools and in government administration. This was to help the infant Republic of Indonesia after 1945. Third, they mobilised young Indonesians to support the Japanese war effort. Various schemes were created to provide military training for young people. This military training proved invaluable when Indonesia had to confront the re-occupying Dutch forces between 1946 and 1949. Fourth, they freed nationalist leaders from jail, including

Sukarno, on the condition that they supported the war effort. Sukarno and other nationalists used every opportunity to nurture a sense of being Indonesian, using all the propaganda tools placed at their disposal by the Japanese.

By the end of 1944 it was clear to the Japanese that they were losing the Pacific War. As a consequence, they determined to make it as difficult as possible for the western powers to re-occupy their former colonies. In Indonesia they began to promote moves towards independence, encouraging nationalists to work out a desirable constitutional framework. Some Indonesians were alarmed at the prospect of obtaining independence courtesy of the Japanese, believing that this would cause the Allied powers to view an independent Indonesia as a puppet regime, thereby playing into the hands of the Dutch whose Netherlands Indies Administration had spent the war years in Brisbane planning to re-occupy Indonesia as soon as the war was over. When the atomic bombs brought the Pacific War to an end, these people prevailed on Sukarno and his fellow nationalist leaders to unilaterally declare independence. The Republic of Indonesia was born on 17 August 1945 at a simple flag raising ceremony in Jakarta.

The Revolution

The Netherlands rejected this declaration of independence, asserting that it was the legitimate government of Indonesia. The Netherlands began its reoccupation of Indonesia in the middle of 1946 and quickly gained control of most of the towns and cities. The Republic of Indonesia government retreated to the principality of Yogyakarta in Central Java. Over the next four years the Indonesians fought the Dutch on two fronts. First, a guerrilla war which quickly bogged down thousands of Dutch troops and prevented the Dutch from holding the countryside. Second, a diplomatic offensive focussed on pressuring the United States to withdraw Marshall Plan aid from the Netherlands and on urging the newly created United Nations to support its independence. In December 1949 an agreement was finally reached between the Republic of Indonesia and the Netherlands bringing the war to an end and formally recognising the end of Dutch colonial rule.

Many western observers in 1950 argued that Indonesia would not survive very long, in the face of regionalism and cultural and ethnic diversity. In retrospect they greatly underestimated the enormous sense of being Indonesian which had been created among a broad cross-section of people by what Indonesians called their revolution. Having to fight for their independence gave at least the Indonesian elites a strong sense of nationalism. Above all, the Revolution saw the emergence of a strong Indonesian army, with a firm ideological commitment to maintaining national unity and to taking a leading role in the development of their society.

As a result of three years of Japanese occupation and four years of warfare with the Dutch, the Indonesian economy was devastated. The economic infrastructure was in tatters, most of the little industry that had existed in 1941 was in ruins and productivity in the plantations and on the farms had regressed to well below pre-war levels. Under-employment in the urban areas was a massive problem, essential services simply didn't work and in the countryside growing population pressure on the land led to lower per capita outputs and a steady stream of migrants to the already overcrowded towns and cities. Added to this was the problem of what to do with the hundreds of thousands of people who had given years of their lives as guerrillas fighting the Dutch. They feared demobilisation when there was little prospect of gainful employment. In 1950 revolutionary elan was high and expectations of the fruits of independence were even higher. The tragedy was that no government in the 1950s could possibly have satisfied these expectations.

Indonesia after Independence

On the eve of independence Indonesian political elites were agreed that Indonesia should be a unitary state and should have Indonesian as its national language. Apart from this they were united on little else. The twenty years between 1945 and 1965 in Indonesia was a period of de-colonisation when four broad groups struggled for control of the state. First, were those who wanted a multi-party parliamentary democracy. Second, those who wanted some kind of consensus parliamentary system, arguing that western liberal democracy was an imported idea not suited to Indonesian cultural and political values. Third, those who wanted some kind of marxist state – the communists were the most visible and strongest but there were other groups who wanted a liberal marxist state or a democratic socialist state. Fourth, those who wanted a state based in some way on Islam, ranging from those who wanted an Islamic state to those who wanted the state merely to reflect Islamic values. These broad divisions can be traced back to debates within nationalist circles since the 1910s. They had not been resolved by 1945, though at that time the marxists and the Muslim groups were in the weakest position.

The Indonesian army has generally supported the second group among the Indonesian elite – those who wanted a consensus political system. The army leadership has consistently seen the army as the major force behind the Indonesian Republic's defeat of the Dutch and because of this believes it has a special role in post-independence Indonesia. Its leaders have talked since the early 1950s of the army's 'dual function' – to defend the nation from external threats or internal subversion as well as to be the engine of development and the protector of the Revolution. The army has always been suspicious of politicians. Its involvement in politics is very different from that of armies elsewhere in Asia,

Africa and Latin America, which on seizing power invariably promise to return to civilian rule as soon as possible. The Indonesian army has made no such commitment. It venerates its origins as a people's army, is proud of its close ties with rural people during the guerrilla campaign against the Dutch, and believes it is more able than any other group to generate and manage the transformation of Indonesian society.

While the army was an important force in Indonesian politics in the 1950s, it became the dominant force only after the events of 30 September 1965 – the coup attempt. These events were the major turning-point in post-independence Indonesian history. There has been a great deal of debate as to what actually happened. The conflict between competing political groups in Indonesia since 1945 had become more intense by the 1960s. Many observers, both Indonesian and foreign, believed that the Indonesian Communist Party was becoming dangerously strong and might shortly be in a position to take over the state. Others were concerned about the growing strength of the armed forces, much more centralised and united in purpose by the early 1960s.

The political instability in Indonesia heightened further in 1965 with rumours of Sukarno being terminally ill and of both the PKI and the armed forces preparing for a coup. On 30 September 1965 a group of lower level army officers declared the overthrow of the Indonesian government. The next day the PKI's official newspaper threw its support behind them. Within twenty four hours the strategic army reserve in Jakarta, under the command of General Suharto, had put down the coup and arrested its leaders.

Over the next six months the army vigorously searched out members of the communist party, whom it blamed for the failed coup and for the murder of six generals. At least 400,000 people were killed in that six month period, mostly in rural Java and Bali. In the aftermath of the events of 30 September 1965 one of the principal political forces since 1945, the communist party, was destroyed. Since 1965 the military-dominated government led by General and now President Suharto has restructured Indonesian politics. It calls itself the 'New Order' government, as opposed to the 'Old Order' of Sukarno's presidency.

Independent Indonesia began as a liberal democracy – with a multi-party parliamentary system, a free and diverse press and with freedom of organisation for voluntary groups, including labour unions. However, its populist President, Sukarno, had argued against western-style multi-party parliamentary democracy since the 1920s (what he called '50 per cent plus one democracy'). He argued that it was not in accordance with Indonesian cultural values which stressed harmony and consensus. Sukarno was a strong advocate of 'democracy with leadership': so too was the army. When parliamentary democracy faltered in the mid 1950s – with widespread discontent with the failure of the revolution to produce prosperity for all – Sukarno marshalled like-minded forces. 'Guided Democracy' between 1959 and 1965 balanced political party representation in parliament with representatives from 'functional groups' – defined as the armed forces, workers, peasants, Muslim scholars and numerous minority groups. The armed forces functional group – called GOLKAR – quickly became the strongest.

Since 1965 the 'New Order' government has openly fostered Golkar. Elections have been held every five years since 1971, but they have been carefully managed. Golkar has been provided with government funds and the bureaucratic and military apparatus swung behind it. Candidates put forward by all political parties are vetted by a government committee and tough electoral rules applied. Not surprisingly, Golkar has won two-thirds or more of the votes in each of the elections.

One issue more than any other has dominated Indonesian political life over the past two decades. This is the government's insistence that pancasila become the sole ideological basis of all political and social organisations. Pancasila is the five principles first enunciated by Sukarno in 1945 as the basis for Indonesian public life: belief in one God; national unity; humanitarianism; democracy based on consensus and representation; and social justice. It is a vague, syncretic philosophy, but its very obscurity allows for many interpretations.

With the Communist Party destroyed, the army, the government and much of the western educated elite have seen a revitalised Islam as the greatest threat to their control of the State. Suharto's government has been determined to inculcate pancasila philosophy throughout the country. The consensus political system, for example, is called pancasila democracy. All school and university students must pass examinations in pancasila, as must civil servants and members of the armed forces. The intention is to remove from the Indonesian political agenda what the government sees as the evils of liberal democracy, Marxism and militant Islam.

The debate in the last decades is not the first time the issue has been heatedly discussed. In mid 1945 the committee of politicians preparing the way for independence after the defeat of Japan were most strongly divided on the role of Islam in independent Indonesia. Many Muslim politicians demanded that Islam be the official religion while others demanded an Islamic state. However, the majority of western educated Indonesians who dominated the nationalist movement from the 1920s were philosophically committed to a secular state, a commitment strengthened by their understanding of the religious diversity in Indonesia. Not only is there a significant Christian minority and a small number of Buddhists and Hindus, but the majority of Indonesians who regard themselves as Muslims reject Islamic fundamentalism.

Some Muslims have never abandoned their desire for Islam to be the basis of the Indonesian state. Other Muslims, while not wanting an Islamic state, have been increasingly critical of what they see as the moral pollution of westernisation. There was an Islamic revival in the 1970s and 1980s, which, in part, reflected the impact of the Iranian revolution and the general resurgence of revivalist Islam in the Middle East on Muslims throughout the world. Many tens of thousands of Indonesians make the pilgrimage to Mecca each year and while there are influenced by these revivalist ideas. It is important to see the great diversity of thinking amongst those Indonesians who identify themselves as part of an Islamic community. The vast majority accept the pancasila state, or at least accept that because of its religious diversity Indonesia can never be an Islamic state, and within this overall philosophical framework are striving to develop political, social and economic policies which reflect their religious values.

Suharto's government has steadily de-politicised Indonesian society. The press is subject to formal and informal controls and the state-operated television network is under firm control with bland news and information services reflecting government views. Magazine publishing is also licensed and books cannot be published without a government permit. The result is a system of self-censorship whereby editors and publishers err on the side of caution in order to avoid the risk of being closed down or of having books and magazines seized. On many occasions the government has withdrawn the right to publish for lengthy periods or permanently closed down publications.

Despite this authoritarianism, there is a considerable amount of debate on major social, economic and political issues. Writers and editors have learned the art of subtlety and innuendo and of pushing criticism just so far. The carefully worded editorial or commentary in daily newspapers is a major method of airing sensitive topics. Cartoonists frequently make critical comments in pictures that could not be made in words – indeed Indonesian newspapers and magazines have fostered talented cartoonists able to make subtle but telling social comment. In the world of literature critics of Indonesian society are also by no means silent.

When the New Order government of President Suharto came to power in 1965 the Indonesian economy was in chaos, inflation was rampant and the social and economic infrastructure had just about collapsed. Much has been achieved in the nearly three decades since then. There has been sustained economic growth, averaging around six per cent per annum, inflation has been brought under control, the economic infrastructure had been enormously improved and there have been sustained efforts to tackle some of the long-standing fundamental problems of the economy.

Rice is the staple food in the Indonesian diet, yet Indonesia was a net importer of rice from the late 19th century until the 1980s. Despite the intricate rice terraces, large-scale irrigation and enormous labour inputs, the productivity of Indonesian rice farmers steadily declined in the 1950s and 1960s. With a remorselessly increasing population the result was a reduction in rice consumption per person and the substitution of less nutritious foods such as cassava. All this has changed since 1979, with dramatic improvements in crop yields and per capita output. In 1983 Indonesia produced its first rice surplus for perhaps one hundred years. The dramatic turn-around in rice production is a result of the Indonesian government's successful agricultural policies. While many developing countries have ignored agriculture in favour of industrial and urban development, the Indonesian government has poured money and expertise into improving agricultural output. The result is considerably increased productivity and the development of agri-businesses for the export of primary products and processed foods.

Successful agricultural policies are the base on which resource development and industrial policies have been constructed. With the gradual opening in the 1990s of huge coal mines in eastern Kalimantan, Indonesia has become a major coal exporter. In the 1970s and early 1980s economic development depended on revenue derived from the export of oil, boosted by the price hikes imposed by OPEC. As the price of oil fell in the 1980s Indonesia was forced to review its economic policies. The result was a steady liberalisation and internationalisation of the economy with stress on securing international investment and developing export oriented manufacturing industries. In the last two decades Indonesia has moved from an import substitution policy in the manufacturing sector to an export oriented policy. It is now a major textile, footwear and clothing exporter and a growing exporter of consumer products. The economic growth of the past thirty years shows every sign of continuing in the decades ahead, promising to move Indonesia into the ranks of the 'Newly Industrialising Economies'.*

In the mid 1990s Indonesia is again at an important point in its history. Economic development since 1965 has been remarkably strong and has moved Indonesia from being one of the poorest countries in the world to the verge of achieving the status of a Newly Industrialising Economy. There is a growing confidence among the Indonesian ruling elite and the middle class that the fundamental social and economic problems of the past half a century or more are on the way to being overcome. They see Indonesia as becoming a significant industrial nation by the early decades of the 21st century. They see Indonesia becoming the major power in Southeast Asia and one of the major countries in Asia.

There are, of course, many Indonesias. The Indonesia of the middle class living in Jakarta is very different from the Indonesia of a farmer in Sulawesi. The Indonesia of strongly Islamic Aceh is very different from the Indonesia of the central Javanese city of Yogyakarta. There is a growing gap between urban and rural dwellers as well as between those who live on Java and those who live elsewhere. There are also widening gaps in the cities between the urban poor and the urban middle class and between the middle class and the wealthy business and power elite.

The New Order government's successful economic policies have accelerated social change. This can be seen in rapid urbanisation, the effects of agri businesses and the green revolution on rural labour needs and most of all, perhaps, in the rapid growth of a middle class.

* Newly Industrialised Economies [NIEs] are sometimes referred to as Newly Industrialised countries [NICs].

The Indonesian middle class is better educated than ever before, more internationally oriented and more articulate than earlier generations. This has led in the last few years to a growing demand for a democratisation of Indonesian political life. There has been much discussion of the need for greater participation in decision making processes, of the need to make pancasila democracy more open and inclusively democratic and on the need for political processes to be more transparent in line with the liberalisation of the economy. This burgeoning middle class holds the key to the direction of political change in the decades ahead. Indonesians are still aware that there is as much diversity in Indonesia as there is unity and that the impressive economic and social gains of the New Order since 1965 have been due in part to the imposition of political stability. In the next decade the Indonesian elite will have to reconcile the demand for greater openness and political participation with the need to maintain social cohesion in order to achieve its economic goals.

TIMELINES

1991: Khamtay Siphandon appointed Prime Minister

1986: Prince Soupanouvong retires

1975: The King abdicates and Prince Soupanouvong becomes President and Kaysone Phomvihan Prime Minister of Lao People's Democratic Republic

1964-75: US bombing of Ho Chi Minh trail and 'secret' war against Pathet Lao forces

1954-64: After the Geneva Conference on Indochina attempts at 'neutralisation' largely unsuccessful

1946: The French return and introduce a number of concessions in the face of conflict in Vietnam and rising hostility from within Lao

1945: Independence declared at the urging of Japan

1893: Franco-Siamese treaty transfers all Lao territory to east of the Mekong River to the French

18th century: Thailand, Myanmar and Vietnam exert control over various parts of the country

1353: Kingdom of Lan Xang with capital at Luang Prabang

7th-13th centuries: Tai migration south from western and northern China

ASEAN FOCUS GROUP

Lao PDR

The Lao People's Democratic Republic or Lao PDR (previously Laos) is about 237,000 sq. km. in land area but has a relatively small population of about 4.4 million in 1994. It is a land-locked country, sharing borders with Thailand, Myanmar, China, Vietnam and Cambodia. Much of it is mountainous, and only about 5 per cent of the land is under continuous cultivation. Primary or secondary jungle (the latter resulting from transient slash-and-burn farming) covers 75 per cent of the land area.

As a nation Lao is a semi-artificial creation of the colonial era. The French devised its borders, cutting through many diverse ethno-linguistic groups. The preponderant Lao lowlanders brought to the emerging nation a long history of bitter division amongst themselves. Lao, as a neighbour of Vietnam, would also be wracked by ideological division and war for thirty years after World War II.

In 1975 the area of Lao was united under one indigenous government for the first time in almost 300 years. The doctrinaire socialism of this government led, however, to economic stagnation and the flight of almost 10 per cent of the country's population across the Mekong river into Thailand. Today the government pursues 'market socialism', welcoming domestic and foreign private enterprise and aid from the capitalist world. But the country's geography, ethnic complexity and turbulent history mean that Laos is starting from far behind most Southeast Asian countries in nation-building and economic development.

The creation of Lao, and its early history

The borders of the modern state of Lao were established by the French colonial government in the late 19th and early 20th centuries. They were based primarily on French strategic and administrative considerations, and only took notice of the region's human geography and traditional political relationships where it suited the French to do so. They sliced through ethnic groupings and historic socio-political ties, arbitrarily determining the future population of the country.

The population of the newly defined territory was relatively sparse – about 819,000 people were counted in 1921 – but nevertheless ethnically and culturally complex. A little over half the population were of Tai ethno-linguistic origin, one result of the great migration which scholars believe brought Tai peoples out of western China into mainland Southeast Asia between the 7th and 13th centuries A.D., and ultimately located Tai stock not only in modern Thailand but also in eastern Myanmar, in Lao and in northwest Vietnam. People of Tai stock in Lao included both the lowland-dwelling Lao and a number of upland-dwelling groups of the northern provinces, such as the Lu, Tai Neua and Black, Red and White Tai (so named for the principal colours in their womens' traditional costumes). Today all these people are grouped as lowlander Lao or 'Lao Loum'.

The lowlander Lao became the dominant force in the region, politically, culturally and economically, but their political structures were not strongly integrated. In the mountainous terrain rivalries of family and clan flourished. Four series of rapids on the Mekong River, with lengthy stretches of water between them, focussed Lao society around three distinct centres, from north to south Luang Prabang, Vientiane (Vieng Chan) and Champassak. The Tai peoples of the uplands were even less politically integrated, although the villages of each group were organised into small principalities (*muong*) presided over by leaders of dominant clans.

The second most substantial ethnolinguistic grouping were upland-dwellers of Mon-Khmer origin, presumably descendants of the peoples who had settled the region before Tai immigration. The Tai-speakers referred to them disparagingly as 'Kha' (slaves); today they are grouped as upland Lao or 'Lao Theung'. Both terms encompass many self-consciously distinct communities with their own names for themselves. Political organisation beyond village level was rare in these communities, but occasionally they could unite, under particularly charismatic chieftains, to oppose lowlander exploitation.

Amongst the smaller ethno-linguistic groupings the most notable by the time of French boundary-drawing were peoples with languages of Tibeto–Burman origin, today grouped as 'Lao Soung' and including the Hmong and Yao, or Mon. (The Hmong resented the lowlander term for them, Meo, which means 'savage'.) These peoples began to migrate into the area as recently as the late 18th or early 19th centuries and settled on upper mountain slopes where amongst other crops they grew the opium poppy. The Hmong shared a myth of a future Hmong kingdom, but for most practical purposes political organisation was rare beyond the level of village chief.

Human settlement in the region is known to date back many centuries B.C. The most famous evidence of the region's pre-history consists of the huge stone mortuary jars found on the north-central Xieng Khouang plateau, which have given the area the name 'Plain of Jars'. Little is known about the society which created the jars, which date from the last centuries B.C. into the early Christian era. The known history of the region follows from the Tai migrations mentioned above. In the 13th century Tai peoples constructed their first states, drawing together hitherto tribal communities under rulers claiming quasi-divine authority and kingly status. Examples of such states were Chiang Mai and Sukhotai (both located in what is now Thailand) and Luang Prabang.

The exact origins of Luang Prabang are shrouded in myth but there in 1316 a royal prince, Fa Ngum, was born. He was brought up in the royal court of the great kingdom of Angkor, which then claimed an empire extending over much of modern Thailand, central and southern Lao, Cambodia and southern Vietnam. Fa

Ngum married a Khmer princess and became a devout Theravada Buddhist. With Khmer forces he brought under his control large areas to Angkor's north and in 1353 established the kingdom of Lan Xang ('a million elephants') with his capital at Luang Prabang.

Initially a tributary of Angkor, Lan Xang became an autonomous kingdom as Angkor declined. For several centuries its power was arguably as significant as the growing Thai state to its west, based on the city of Ayudhya, and the growing Vietnamese state to its east. At its height Lan Xang controlled, at least in loose, tributary fashion, territories considerably more extensive than those of modern Lao, including much of modern Thailand's north and east and reaching into the south of modern China and the northwest of modern Vietnam.

Lan Xang was a Buddhist kingdom and for long periods a renowned centre of Buddhist scholarship. However its Buddhist practices took on a distinctively Lao identity as the religion assimilated the traditional animist beliefs and rituals of the region. Buddhism also acted as a conduit for ideas, Indian in origin, of society as divinely-ordained hierarchy. Lan Xang's polity came broadly to resemble those of its Theravada Buddhist neighbours, the Burmese, Thai and Cambodian states. The king and aristocracy deserved reverence, taxes and services from their subjects because of their superior 'merit' and pious support of Buddhism. Such politico-religious social integration extended only to the lowlander Lao, however. The 'Kha' (uplanders) mostly resisted Buddhism, clinging to their diverse animist beliefs and local independence. And even among the lowlanders Lan Xang's rugged geography and necessarily decentralised administration by regional overlords militated against a lastingly strong state.

Nevertheless Lan Xang weathered internal rivalries, wars with the Thais and Vietnamese, and a generation of Burmese overlordship in the late 16th century. In the 17th century, now with Vientiane as its capital, Lan Xang reached its height under King Souligna Vongsa, who came to the throne in 1637 after defeating four rival claimants and reigned for a remarkable 57 years. He negotiated good relations with the neighbouring states, and within the kingdom gained a reputation for firm, just rule. The first European visitors to Vientiane reported on the city's prosperity and imposing religious buildings.

But, in an act worthy of epic tragedy, Souligna Vongsa refused to intervene when his only son seduced the wife of a senior court official and, under the prevailing law on such matters, was sentenced to death. Souligna Vongsa died in 1694 without a direct heir, and the subsequent rivalries for the throne, exploited by the Vietnamese and Thais, led to the kingdom's irrevocable break-up.

In the early 18th century the cities of Luang Prabang and Vientiane became the capitals of antagonistic states, the latter under Vietnamese patronage. In the south Champassak fell under Thai patronage. In the mid-18th century the Burmese became predatory again, reducing Luang Prabang to subjection and menacing Vientiane. Rather than supporting one another the mutually hostile Lao states encouraged these outside powers to subdue their Lao rivals. The unhappy century closed with Vientiane under Thai overlordship, although Vientiane independently attacked and sacked Luang Prabang in 1791.

In 1805 the Lao prince Chao Anou became ruler at Vientiane, and won Thai and also Vietnamese approval to reintegrate the central and southern provinces. In 1826, however, Chao Anou acted on a rumour (which proved false) that the British were attacking Bangkok. Chao Anou and his forces, eager to join in the humbling of the Thais, almost reached Bangkok before being repelled. Chao Anou fled, ultimately taking shelter from Thai vengeance in Vietnam.

These events opened a decade of devastation for the Vientiane state. In 1828 Thai forces sacked Vientiane and drove many thousands of the population westward into territory under Bangkok control. Vientiane, and Champassak in the south, became minor Thai provinces. Chao Anou was captured by the Thais when he returned to his territory with ineffective Vietnamese backing; he died in Bangkok in 1835, bringing the Vientiane monarchy to an end.

Meanwhile Vietnam was forcefully asserting its claims in the eastern provinces, particularly in Xieng Khouang (the Plain of Jars). The Vietnamese were probably content to take the east while the Thais took the west and south, but in 1833, simultaneously with a Thai–Vietnamese clash in Cambodia, the Thais sent a force against the Vietnamese garrison in Xieng Khouang. The Thais were helped by forces from Luang Prabang, and by a local uprising in Xieng Khouang against the Vietnamese. As with Vientiane the Thais adopted a 'scorched earth' policy in Xieng Khouang, deporting westward up to 80 per cent of the population, although some were able to return later. Thai–Vietnamese warfare continued until 1835, and concluded with the Vietnamese dominant in the east, as they had wished, and the Thais dominant in the western and southern provinces. The surviving northerly kingdom of Luang Prabang prudently acknowledged the overlordship of both its neighbours, but for practical purposes it too was within the Thai orbit.

French conquest and rule, to 1940

The French takeover of Cambodia and Vietnam between the 1860s and 1885 led to keen French interest in the Lao territories for several reasons. They saw the Mekong (wrongly) as a potentially major trade route with China. They also feared Thai interests in the territories, which they believed might be championed (also wrongly as it transpired) by their imperial rival Britain. From the 1870s northern Lao and Vietnam were disturbed by armed bands of renegade Chinese (collectively referred to by the Thai term 'Ho') and the French were anxious to pacify these areas. Finally, by 1885 the French controlled the Vietnamese emperor's claims to overlordship in the Lao territories.

The Thais had been sending armed forces to Luang Prabang and other areas in an attempt to subdue the Ho and confront possible French intervention. But in 1887 they were dramatically outmanoeuvred by the French explorer Auguste Pavie, who rescued the king of Luang Prabang when the Ho attacked and sacked his city. King Un Kham gratefully accepted French protection for his kingdom. Pavie went on to negotiate similar protection for other regional overlords.

In 1893 (with French gunboats menacing Bangkok) Thailand reluctantly signed a Franco-Siamese treaty which transferred to the French all Lao territories east of the Mekong. Further agreements in 1904 and 1907 added to 'Lao' the parts of Sayaboury and Champassak provinces west of the Mekong. However for most of its course through historically Lao territory the Mekong had now become an international frontier. The agreements on other borders with British Burma, China and with French-controlled Vietnam similarly conflicted with the historic settlement patterns and movements of Lao and other people of the region.

The French soon came to regard Lao as a quiet backwater, when they realised that it could offer no rapid economic return of any significance. Most people of the region continued as subsistence farmers, the lowlanders growing wet rice and the uplanders pursuing slash-and-burn cultivation. The colony's most important products became tin, mined by Vietnamese workers, and opium grown by the Hmong and other mountain-dwellers. The tin contributed only a tiny percentage of the total exports of French Indochina (Lao, Vietnam and Cambodia). Opium, on the other hand, became Lao's single greatest revenue earner when purveyed by a French state monopoly throughout Indochina. An illegal opium trade also flourished with China, despite official French efforts at control.

The French administration of Lao (technically now the protected kingdom of Luang Prabang plus nine Lao provinces) was lightly staffed. Much administration was carried out using traditional authority structures and Vietnamese minor officials. Vietnamese public servants, traders and professionals came to predominate in Lao's small urban population; Chinese also came to play a significant role in Lao's trade. Generally the Lao lowlanders accepted the French and other outsiders, but mountain-dwelling groups rose in revolt on several occasions. They were protesting against taxation and corvée demands possibly imposed inequitably, even corruptly, by officials from the traditionally resented lowlands.

Prior to World War II modernisation in Lao was extremely limited. The telegraph and around 5,000 km of roads (mostly unpaved) eased communications, but 90 per cent of the population remained in subsistence agriculture. Health care and other social services were confined to the towns, and no western-style education was available in Lao beyond primary level (most primary education was conducted in the Buddhist temple schools). The Lao elite went to Vietnam or France to acquire an education, returning to form a small royal and aristocratic upper class, and a fledgling Lao middle class composed of public servants, policemen and soldiers, primary teachers and the like.

World War II and the First Indochina War, 1940–1954

In 1940 the Thais, taking advantage of Japanese pressures on the French, occupied with Japanese support the Lao provinces west of the Mekong. (These would be returned to the French in 1947.) However the French retained administrative control in most of Indochina, under an agreement with the Japanese which allowed the free movement of Japanese forces. Thus most of Lao stayed under French supervision until 9 March 1945, when the Japanese interned all French personnel in Indochina.

The war years before March 1945 nevertheless brought significant change. The French, seeking to buttress Lao popular support, began to stimulate Lao nationalist pride. A 'national renovation movement' staged rallies and parades, built schools and other amenities, fostered Lao music, dance and literature, and led to the first Lao newspaper. The first explicitly Lao infantry battalion was formed, under French control, in 1943. As elsewhere in Southeast Asia, therefore, nationalist politicisation was a feature of the war years in Lao, although the Lao movement focussed only on the Lao lowlanders.

After March 1945 the pace quickened. In April the king of Luang Prabang was obliged by the Japanese to repudiate the French and declare Lao 'independent'. In August, when the Japanese surrendered to the Allies, politicised Lao people were split between those who acquiesced in a French return and those who saw the opportunity to set up a genuinely independent state. The latter formed the Lao Issara (Free Lao) and set up a provisional government.

By now, however, an additional complication for Lao nationalism was taking shape. In August/September 1945 Ho Chi Minh's communists seized control in northern Vietnam and set up the Democratic Republic of Vietnam (DRV). Some Lao Issara, seeking allies, established ties with the DRV, which eagerly backed the anti-French movement in Lao. The political contenders in Lao – and the entire population – were about to be sucked into the maelstrom created by the advent of communism in the region and by French – and later American – efforts to eliminate or contain it.

The French recaptured Lao by May 1946, and leading Lao Issara figures fled, some to Bangkok and some to link up with the DRV guerrilla forces (the Vietminh) battling the French in Vietnam. In the late 1940s Lao guerrilla groups developed along the mountainous Lao–Vietnam border, aided by Vietminh know-how and supplies. Significantly, these groups won the support of some uplander communities hitherto alienated from the Lao nationalist movement. The uplanders may have been recruited with some cynicism by the Lao and Vietminh – who primarily viewed the uplanders as important for their strategically valuable territory and local knowledge – but trans-communal nationalist cooperation had at last made a start.

Meanwhile the Lao Issara group in Bangkok was disintegrating. The French, anxious to pacify Lao in order to focus on the conflict in Vietnam, made a series of concessions to Lao feelings which undercut the hostility of many Lao Issara towards the restored French presence. In 1946 the French appointed the Luang Prabang monarch as king of all Lao, and also permitted an elected national assembly, leading to a national government. In 1949 they declared Lao 'independent', though they retained ultimate control of the kingdom's armed forces, foreign policy and finances. The concessions were enough, nevertheless, to woo many Lao Issara back under amnesty.

Notable amongst the returnees was the royal Prince Souvanna Phouma, who became Prime Minister following elections in 1951. However his half-brother, Prince Souphanouvong, in an echo of the country's past history of ruling class dissension, threw in his lot with the Vietminh-backed guerrilla forces. In August 1950 Souphanouvong became Prime Minister of the newly formed Pathet Lao ('Land of the Lao') a front organisation open to all Lao patriots though tightly controlled by committed communists. Another key pioneer Pathet Lao figure, as Defence Minister, was the Lao–Viet communist Kaysone Phomvihan, destined to become Lao's first and long-lasting communist Prime Minister.

By early 1954 Pathet Lao forces controlled large areas of the north and northeast of Lao, including the Plain of Jars and the provincial town of Sam Neua. They had been significantly helped in their advance by major Vietminh incursions into Lao in April 1953 and January 1954. The Pathet Lao was not invited to the Geneva Conference which opened in May 1954, convened by the great powers in the hope of settling the Indochina conflicts, but the Conference recognised Pathet Lao strength and acknowledged its right to administer the territory it held. The Conference called, however, for the integration of the Pathet Lao with the Royal Lao government and armed forces, and for the neutralisation of Lao.

The failure of 'neutralisation', 1954–1964

Following the Geneva Conference the French speedily withdrew from Indochina. In Laos the negotiations for a new, integrated national government would prove tortuous and long. The Pathet Lao was determined to enter a coalition only on strong terms, and was wary of growing American influence in Lao. In Vientiane the moderate Souvanna Phouma was swept aside by United States-supported right-wingers, who had gained the upper hand in the National Assembly and Royal Lao armed forces.

Elections in December 1955 led, however, to Souvanna's return to the prime ministership on a platform of national reconciliation. In August 1956 Souvanna and the Pathet Lao leadership agreed on broad proposals for a 'government of national union'. Elections for 21 extra assembly seats were finally held in May 1958, with parties aligned with the Pathet Lao acquiring 13. Souphanouvong entered the government as a Senior Economic Minister. Another Pathet Lao leader, Phoumi Vongvichit, also acquired a Ministry. The arrangements were a dubious recipe for stability. In June 1958 Souvanna was again forced from office by the rightists, and the succeeding government went on to rule by decree. Souphanouvong and the other leftist deputies were arrested, although they later escaped with the aid of their guards and returned to Pathet Lao territory in the east. Pathet Lao troops who had been awaiting integration with the Royal Lao forces were disarmed, but many of them too escaped back to Pathet Lao territory. By July 1959 guerrilla warfare was again in full swing in the north and northeast. United States aid to the Royal Lao forces sharply increased. Simultaneously CIA personnel began to form 'special forces' in Lao, attracting support among the Hmong in particular. With CIA assistance Hmong opium output began to find vast new markets in South Vietnam, Thailand and beyond.

The conflict increased in complexity in August 1960, when forces led by a young paratroop captain, Kong Le, seized Vientiane and demanded a restoration of neutrality. Souvanna Phouma agreed to return as Prime Minister, and subsequently reached an agreement with Souphanouvong on behalf of the Pathet Lao. In December 1960, however, Royal Lao troops under rightist command stormed Vientiane. Kong Le, his troops and Souvanna fled to the Pathet Lao-controlled Plain of Jars. The communist world and some non-aligned nations like India now upheld Souvanna as Lao rightful Prime Minister. The United States and the West recognised a new military-controlled Vientiane government, technically under another prince, Boun Oum, as Prime Minister.

Despite American intrigue in Lao up to this point, the incoming United States President in January 1961, John Kennedy, concluded that a neutral Lao was desirable. Neutrality would hopefully exclude DRV forces from using the 'Ho Chi Minh Trail', much of which ran through Lao, to reinforce and supply NLF ('Vietcong') forces now fighting the regime in South Vietnam. In May 1961 another Geneva Conference called once more for the neutralisation of Lao. In June the three Lao princes, Boun Oum, Souvanna Phouma, and Souphanouvong agreed to a second attempt at coalition government.

The new government came into existence in July 1962 with Souvanna as Prime Minister. The coalition led a tenuous existence, beset by tension, provocation and assassination until mid-1964 when its Pathet Lao component effectively abandoned it, later dismissing it as a 'United States puppet'. Souvanna held on as Prime Minister, but he and other neutralists were now reduced to irrelevance. Lao was becoming one of the key theatres of war in the sharply escalating conflict in Vietnam.

Lao and the Vietnam conflict, 1964–1975

Secret United States bombing of Pathet Lao areas began in May 1964. By the late 1960s, and into the early 1970s, the bombing was massive, attempting 'saturation' destruction of the manifold branches of the Ho Chi Minh Trail. It created an estimated 750,000 refugees in Lao, and nightmarish conditions for Pathet Lao forces, but it never closed the Trail, or eliminated Pathet Lao headquarters and networks. On the ground, the Royal Lao and 'secret' forces (and also substantial Thai forces) engaged each year in a 'dry season' war with the Pathet Lao. For many years the pattern of territories held by the opposing forces did not alter significantly. By 1972, however, the Pathet Lao was beginning to gain ground, backed by an increasingly optimistic and well-armed DRV.

In Paris the DRV was engaged in serious peace talks with the United States, which would lead to the January 1973 agreements under which the United States withdrew its ground troops from Vietnam. The Pathet Lao, pursuing a policy parallel to that of the DRV, offered in 1972 to talk with the Vientiane government 'without preconditions'. In February 1973 the two sides reached an 'Agreement on the Restoration of Peace and Reconciliation in Laos'.

The agreement provided for cessation of hostilities, after which the two sides would administer their respective territories, and for the withdrawal of foreign troops. The United States and Thais withdrew their military personnel, though the DRV continued to use the Ho Chi Minh Trail. Further detailed agreements led to the formation of two bodies on which both the Vientiane government and the Pathet Lao were represented. These were the Provisional Government of National Union, in which Souvanna Phouma became Prime Minister, and a National Political Consultative Council (NPCC), of which Souphanouvong became Chairman.

The NPCC subsequently committed itself to the retention of the monarchy and to generally liberal political and economic principles. Pathet Lao government Ministers also acted moderately, reassuring many Lao people. The Pathet Lao goal remained, however, full takeover of government, and the circumstances seemed to be favouring the achievement of that goal. Rightist morale was sinking as the United States, step by step, wound back its commitments in Indochina. Corruption and self-seeking – which had long been debilitating factors in the Royal Lao government area – intensified as fears grew that the United States aid bonanza was coming to an end.

Even so the Pathet Lao moved cautiously when, in April 1975, communist forces toppled the regimes in Saigon and Phnom Penh. Pathet Lao troops engaged the Hmong 'secret army', but in the lowlands the Pathet Lao relied on staging a 'popular revolution'. In April and May, mass demonstrations against United States properties and Lao rightists led to the wind-back of all American activity other than diplomatic representation, and propelled the flight from Lao of people identified with the former Vientiane government. The flight intensified when the Royal Lao forces were taken over by a pro-Pathet Lao commander in August. In November, following further demonstrations, the King abdicated and Souvanna Phouma stepped down as Prime Minister.

On the 1st and 2nd December 1975 a 'National Congress of Peoples Representatives' voted unanimously to establish the Lao People's Democratic Republic, to be governed by the Lao People's Revolutionary Party. Prince Souphanouvong became the new republic's first President (he would retire in 1986). Kaysone Phomvihane became Prime Minister, a position he would retain until 1991, when Khamtay Siphandone succeeded him as Prime Minister.

Lao since 1975

After 1975 the new government imposed doctrinaire socialist policies on Lao. State Trading Organisations replaced private trade, and Lao's small industries were nationalised. The properties of 'traitors' were expropriated. Political and social discourse became rigidly controlled, and perceived opponents of the regime were eliminated or consigned to 're-education' centres. In 1978 cooperativisation of agriculture began. These policies aggravated the conditions created by 30 years of political upheaval and war, the withdrawal of United States aid and an economic blockade imposed by Thailand. The declining economic situation and the political oppression led to the exodus as refugees of as much as 10 per cent of the population. By 1979 Lao had lost the majority of its educated and skilled people.

Cooperativisation – the policy which most directly affected the majority of the peasant population – met with passive but intense opposition. Harvest yields were catastrophically less than hoped for, and in mid-1979 the policy was abruptly dropped. This about-turn heralded a series of measures which would gradually free up the country's economy. In November 1979 private production was again encouraged, and state enterprises were obliged to include in their goals efficiency, productivity and profit. In 1982 a reorganisation of government left the old guard in supreme control but introduced 'technocrats' at vice-ministerial level, decentralised some decision-making, and liberalised foreign trade, private investment and joint state-private enterprise.

These and later changes to the command economy provoked some tensions within the ruling group, but in the late 1980s and early 1990s the collapse of Soviet and European communism, the resulting loss of aid, and the growing economic liberalisation in Vietnam and China, produced decisive moves towards a market economy. However Lao remains a one-party, theoretically socialist, state. Party diktat can over-ride law and institutionalised procedures.

With its small population, lack of infrastructure and land-locked position, Lao is unlikely to shake off quickly its status as one of Southeast Asia's poorest countries, in spite of its now very liberal policies on foreign investment Subsistence farming is likely to remain the chief user of labour for some time, and the chief means of survival for most Lao people. However Lao does have potential for modest economic growth. Foreign companies are now heavily involved in developing a number of hydro-electric projects, principally to sell power to Thailand. Other areas of potential development are mining, commercial agriculture, tourism and limited areas of manufacturing.

Meanwhile Lao's infrastructure is improving, with various forms of international assistance. An Australian-built bridge across the Mekong, which linked Lao and Thailand by road in 1994, plus the expansion and upgrading of roads within Lao, mean that it is becoming possible to drive from Singapore to Beijing, via Lao. And yet many Lao see their country's future as a transport hub, linking northeast Thailand with the Vietnamese port of Da Nang on an east–west axis as well as southern China with Thailand, Malaysia and Singapore on the north-south axis. Some Lao people fear the social and environmental consequences of development in Lao, and economic domination by their powerful neighbours. The government will need to handle development with sensitivity as Lao is drawn inexorably into the dynamic economic currents sweeping through the rest of Southeast Asia.

TIMELINES

1993: Goverment challenges power and privileges of royal state rulers and their families

1981: Dr Mahathir elected Prime Minister and adopts 'Look East' policy

1971: Tunku Abdul Razak elected Prime Minister and New Economic Policy period begins

1969: Riots between Chinese and Malays

1963: Malaysia formed with Tunku Abdul Rahman elected first Prime Minister

1957: Independence granted

1948: Federation of Malaya formed and state of emergency declared after Communist Party of Malaya attempts revolution

1941-45: Japanese occupation

1874: Pangkor Treaty with Perak sets scene for British to extend control throughout peninsular

1843-1917: 'White Rajah' period in Sarawak

1824: British acquire Melaka and form Straits Settlements with Penang and Singapore

1641: Johore with assistance from the Dutch in Java oust Portuguese

1400: Melaka established by refugees from Sri Vijaya which was under siege from the Javanese kingdom of Majapahit

7th-14th centuries: Sri Vijaya imperial state encompassing Peninsular Malaysia, Sumatra, western Java and western Borneo

ASEAN FOCUS GROUP

Malaysia

More than 60 ethnic or culturally differentiated groups can be found in Malaysia's population of just under 20 million, but the most crucial population division is that between Bumiputera and non-Bumiputera people. The Bumiputeras are those with cultural affinities indigenous to Peninsular and Bornean Malaysia and the immediate region. Malays constitute the principal Bumiputera group and account for around 55 per cent of Malaysia's population. Non-Bumiputeras are people whose cultural affinities lie outside Malaysia and its region – principally people of Chinese and Indian descent. Chinese constitute about 32 per cent of Malaysia's population and Indians about 8 per cent.

The Malays have a long history and, since the 15th century, an Islamic culture in which they take pride. In the colonial era, however, their cultural world – extending across the Malay Peninsula and Indonesian Archipelago – was divided by Western colonial powers. In British Malaya and northern Borneo Malays were relegated to minor social roles and virtually excluded from the foreign-financed modernising economy, which utilised immigrant labour. Malaysia's history since World War II has been primarily the story of the reassertion of Malay primacy without precipitating serious racial discord.

Malaysia's stability has enabled vast economic growth, particularly in the 1970s and 1980s. The stability has been at the expense, however, of some elements of the democratic system with which Malaysia began as an independent nation. Malay advancement has also had an ironic political consequence – nowadays rifts and rivalries within the Malay community need as much adroit political management as the differences between Malaysia's ethnic groups.

Early history

The early history of the territories which now form Malaysia is shadowy, a matter of cryptic archaeological clues and obscure references in Chinese and other written sources. The limited evidence suggests, however, that in the first millennium A.D. both the Malay Peninsula and the northern Borneo coast were important landfalls for merchant vessels involved in the great maritime trading networks that linked Southeast Asia with Africa, the Middle East, India and China. Port cities arose on the Peninsula and on Borneo as they did elsewhere in Southeast Asia, offering merchants safe harbourage, trans-shipment facilities and collection points for the region's prized commodities – gold, tin and other minerals, rare woods, resins and other jungle produce, tortoiseshell, cowries and other marine produce, and – supremely – spices.

Malay history is often seen as beginning, however, in southern Sumatra. Scholars believe that between the 7th and 14th centuries the Palembang region of southern Sumatra was the focus of a major maritime empire. They called the central imperial state Sri Vijaya, though evidence about it is fragmentary and inconclusive. Close by Sri Vijaya, and at times possibly its capital, was a place called Melayu, perhaps the cradle of Malay culture. The Sri Vijayan empire at its height probably dominated the trade of most of Sumatra, the Malay Peninsula, western Java and western Borneo. It enjoyed Chinese and Indian patronage and, like most of Southeast Asia in the first millennium A.D., it borrowed and adapted Indian culture and religion. Its religion was probably a variant of Mahayana Buddhism.

Melaka and Malay culture: the 15th century

In the 14th century Sri Vijaya was suppressed by the Javanese kingdom of Majapahit, a rival for control of Archipelago trade. Refugees from Sri Vijaya moved north to the Riau-Lingga islands, then on to Singapore island and other locations before eventually founding the city of Melaka (Malacca). The Sejarah Melayu (the 'Malay Annals') has it that their leader, Sultan Iskandar, was out hunting one day when one of his dogs was kicked by a mousedeer, normally the most timid and tremulous of animals. He took the mousedeer's courage as a fine omen for the new city.

Founded about 1400, Melaka would enjoy a century of greatness, both as a major trade centre and as a great cultural centre. Melakan Malay culture would be admired and adopted in many parts of the Peninsula and Archipelago, including northern Borneo. Tales of Melaka's wealth and influence would reach even Europe, making it a prime target for conquest when Westerners sailed into the Eastern seas.

Melaka's trading prowess was based on a number of factors. Its position was excellent, commanding the busy Strait which took its name. Its rulers established efficient and secure conditions for traders, on land and on nearby sea lanes. Potential rival ports were brought into a tributary relationship to Melaka. At the height of its power Melaka probably dominated the Peninsula as far north as Perak (in the north of what is now known as Malaysia), the Riau-Lingga Archipelago and most of Sumatra's east coast.

At the same time Melaka took care to become a tributary of powers greater than itself – most importantly China but also Majapahit and the Thai state of Ayudhya. Sending tribute to such powers meant no loss of independence in practical terms, but did encourage such powers to send their traders to Melaka. A Chinese community quickly settled and became a feature of Melakan society, making Chinese people a part of Malaysian history effectively from its beginning.

At some time early in the 15th century Melaka's rulers adopted Islam, and this too contributed to the city's success, making it a favoured destination for Arab and Indian Muslim traders. Although some smaller ports in northern Sumatra preceded Melaka in turning to Islam, Melaka's conversion triggered the Islamisation of the Peninsula and Archipelago. Over the next century, port city after port city would adopt the religion of the most powerful, prestigious and culturally dynamic of their number. Along with its religion the port cities also tended to adopt the Melakan form of government – a blend of Middle Eastern Islamic forms with Indian forms brought from Sri Vijaya – and the language of Melaka, Malay. Malay thus became the most widely understood language in the region. In the 20th century Malay would become not only the language of Malaysia and Brunei but, as the language of trade in the Archipelago for centuries, it would form the basis of the Indonesian national language.

The golden age of Melaka ended abruptly in August 1511, when after a month's siege the city fell to the superior guns of the Portuguese. The Portuguese hoped to take command of Melaka's trading networks, particularly its control over spices from the Moluccas. However, while the European newcomers had the power to take control of the city and the Strait it overlooked, they lacked the resources to control the entire region and compel trade to continue at Melaka. Their posture as enemies of Islam scarcely helped. The Portuguese coup probably only stimulated the Malay trading world, as other port cities vied to take the fallen city's place, championing with new urgency Melaka's former religion and culture.

One state exemplifying this effect was Brunei, a port city dominating Borneo's north coast (then encompassing not only modern Brunei but also the Malaysian states of Sarawak and Sabah). Chinese records suggest that a port state, 'P'o – ni', existed in the region from the 5th century. About 1514, Brunei's rulers accepted Islam, emphasised their connections with Melaka's former ruling dynasty, and began to develop a 'Brunei-Malay' culture.

A threatening world: the 16th to 18th centuries

Following the loss of Melaka, its ruling elite and their followers eventually established the sultanate of Johor, commanding the southern Peninsula and Riau islands. Elsewhere on the Peninsula other states flourished, usually claiming legitimacy through connection with the former Melaka and paying tribute to Johor.

In spite of Portuguese attempts to subdue Johor it prospered in the late 16th and early 17th centuries, especially when the Dutch arrived on the scene. Basing themselves in Java, the Dutch saw Johor as a useful counterweight to the Portuguese at Melaka and developed trading arrangements with the sultanate. In 1641 Johor helped the Dutch oust the Portuguese from Melaka, which then became a minor, outlying base in a growing Dutch empire.

The Dutch had considerably greater resources than the Portuguese had been able to deploy – and also, by the 17th century, greater resources than another northwestern Borneo the sultanate of Brunei had to come to terms with the adventurous and fearsome 'head-hunter' warriors who spearheaded the migrations of Dayak (Iban) communities. Rival Brunei chiefs often struck up alliances with rival Dayak groups, sharpening conflict in the sultanate. Both the Bugis and Minangkabau migrants of the 18th century would, over time, adopt Malay-Muslim custom and to all intents and purposes merge with Malay society. The Dayaks would be tamed under British colonial rule but would always retain their distinctive, non-Muslim, cultures.

Other factors would also increase instability in the 18th century Malay world. The growing power of the British in India reoriented the trading patterns of the sub-continent. British traders in Southeast Asia were often welcomed as potential allies against other Western or local powers, but their cargoes, featuring opium and firearms, were deadly. Meanwhile, Chinese doing business in the region tended increasingly to favour linkages with Westerners rather than local governments. They were thus heralding the 'middle men' roles which Chinese would hold between the indigenous peoples and the Western colonial regimes of the 19th and 20th centuries.

On the Peninsula the Thais also became a major intrusive force in the later 18th century. The Thai kingdom of Ayudhya had claimed sovereignty on the Peninsula since the 14th century, and often exacted tribute from the more northerly states. In 1767 the city of Ayudhya was destroyed by the Burmese, but from 1782 a new Thai dynasty arose – the Chakri (still Thailand's royal house) – with a new capital, Bangkok. The early Chakri monarchs were determined to assert Thai royal authority more firmly than ever before. In the late 18th and early 19th centuries the northern Malay states of Patani, Kelantan, Kedah, Perak and to a lesser extent Trengganu all experienced Thai pressures.

Patani effectively lost its independence and was absorbed within the Thai administrative sphere, thus creating a permanent Malay-Muslim minority in Buddhist Thailand. The other states continued as tributaries, running their own affairs, but Bangkok's enforcement of tribute payments and other decrees could be brutal and destructive.

In 1786 the ruler of Kedah, hoping to win an ally against the Thais, ceded Penang island to the (British) East India Company, which was looking for a safe harbour and trading base in the region. In 1800 a strip of territory on the mainland opposite the island was also ceded. The Kedah rulers merely acquired an annual pension for the ceded territory; to their chagrin the Company firmly refused to become involved in their struggles with the Thais. However the first step had been taken towards British occupation of the Peninsula.

The British advance: the 19th century

In 1819 the East India Company acquired Singapore island from Johor. In

1824 an Anglo–Dutch treaty delivered Melaka into British hands too, as part of a delineation by the two European powers of their respective spheres of influence in maritime Southeast Asia. Making the Melaka Straits a frontier, the British took the Peninsula as their preserve, while the Dutch took Sumatra and all islands to the south of Singapore. Northern Borneo was not mentioned, though British interests would claim later, in the face of Dutch protests, that the terms of the 1824 treaty made that area a British sphere of influence too.

The 1824 treaty effectively determined the future boundaries of the British and Dutch colonial possessions in the region, and also of the nation states which would emerge from the colonial era, Malaysia and Indonesia. In the 1820s, however, the British had no intention of entangling themselves in the Peninsula. They were satisfied with the Straits Settlements, as Singapore, Melaka and Penang became known from 1826. (The Straits Settlements remained under the East India Company until 1858, when the government of British India took over. In 1867 they were transferred to the control of the British Colonial Office.)

The Straits Settlements boomed, and inevitably business interests there, Western and Chinese, became interested in exploiting the Peninsular states. The question arose of whether the states' traditional administrative structures would be able to cope with the pressures arising from the new economic ventures. The rulers of Johor, closest to Singapore, proved fully equal to a major expansion of Chinese commercial agriculture in their state, principally in pepper and gambier. Kedah was also well governed and able to cope with spill-over pressures from Penang. The ruling groups of other states proved less adroit.

Pahang experienced civil war between 1858 and 1863, partly over the spoils arising from expanding ventures in mining and jungle produce. More seriously, endemic feuding developed within the ruling classes of the western Peninsular states of Perak, Selangor and Negeri Sembilan over the control of vast tin deposits, which began to be worked in the 1840s. The tin was mined by Chinese labourers controlled by secret societies. Rival Malay chiefs aligned themselves and their followers with the forces of rival secret societies. Rival business houses in the Straits Settlements backed one side or the other with money and guns. By the 1860s these states were in anarchy. Demands for official British intervention grew.

In 1874, one of the leading Malay disputants in Perak and the Governor of the Straits Settlements put their names to the Pangkor Treaty. The treaty recognised the former as Sultan, but insisted, crucially, that he should accept a British Resident in his state, whose advice 'must be asked and acted upon on all questions other than those touching Malay religion and custom'. The British interpreted broadly which matters were unrelated to 'Malay religion and custom', so taking effective control of most financial and administrative matters.

The Pangkor Treaty thus pioneered the formula by which the British would achieve authority in the Peninsular states. Constitutionally the states would be 'protected' sovereign states, retaining their rulers. Practically the Resident (or in some cases 'Adviser') could extend his control as far as the British wished. By the 1880s not only Perak but Selangor, Negeri Sembilan and Pahang were under such a system. In 1896 these states became the 'FMS' (Federated Malay States) with their federal administrative centre at Kuala Lumpur, a young city growing out of a tin-mining camp.

In 1909, Thailand relinquished its imperial claims to the northern Malay states of Kedah, Perlis, Kelantan and Trengganu, and Britain moved to install Advisers in these states. In 1914 Johor was also obliged to accept an Adviser, despite its long record of satisfactory administration. Johor and the northern states were not brought under federal administration and became the 'UMS' (Unfederated Malay States). Even so, by the second decade of the 20th century the British had begun to talk about 'Malaya' – that term disguising a constitutional hotch-potch of Crown colony (the Straits Settlements) and nine protected sovereign states, four of them federated and five not.

In northern Borneo, meanwhile, two unique – indeed eccentric – expressions of British colonialism had emerged at the expense of the sultanate of Brunei. Brunei was impoverished in the 19th century and further weakened by bitter factionalism within its ruling class. In 1840 a British adventurer, James Brooke, was recruited to quell a revolt in the Sarawak river region, at the sultanate's western extremity. Between 1841 and 1843 Brooke acquired full possession of the region and made the town of Kuching (meaning cat in the Malay language) his base. From there he and his nephew and successor as 'White Raja' Charles Brooke (ruler 1868 – 1917) expanded their territory eastward, establishing Sarawak's final borders shortly after the turn of the century. Brunei would be left as two small enclaves within Sarawak.

Several factors propelled Brooke expansionism, the most important being Brunei's poverty and the dispersal of power in the sultanate, which made the piecemeal acquisition of territory for small sums relatively easy. In addition, in the 1840s the British navy saw James Brooke as an ally in its efforts to stamp out piracy in Southeast Asian waters. Brooke was backed on several occasions by intimidating displays of British naval power when dealing with Brunei. From the 1850s British support was withheld from the Brookes, for fear that such private imperial ventures might embarrass Britain, but this made no difference. The Brookes had their own source of intimidating power – large contingents of Dayak warriors. They also had an idealistic rationale for their advance, believing that they were developing a unique experiment in efficient and benevolent government for native peoples.

Competition would add further urgency to Charles' expansionism from the 1870s. In 1877–78 a British business consortium acquired the rights to most of the territory of Sabah, to Brunei's east, from Brunei and from the sultanate of Sulu in what is now the southern Philippines. (Here was the origin of a dormant but still unresolved dispute over Sabah between the Philippines and Malaysia. The Philippines, as successor state to Sulu, claims that Sulu merely 'leased' rather than 'ceded' its rights in Sabah.) By 1881 the business consortium had persuaded the British government to charter a company, financed by shares, to administer the Sabahan territories, hopefully at a profit. Thus Sabah became 'British North Borneo', governed by the British North Borneo Chartered Company.

Charles Brooke was outraged. During the 1880s and 1890s there was fierce competition between him and the Chartered Company over the Brunei territories that remained unceded. In 1888 Britain moved to guarantee that at least the core lands of the sultanate should survive, making Brunei a British protectorate. In 1906 Brunei received a British Adviser, with powers similar to those of Residents in the Peninsular states. By then Brunei had new-found economic significance; large oil deposits had been located in Brunei Bay.

The colonial era

On the Peninsula the extension of British control met with some opposition but it was soon quelled. The British now set about creating an environment for economic expansion. The tin industry which had boomed in the 1840s continued to grow, moving from Chinese to Western control in the 20th century when capital-intensive mechanisation of the industry arrived. In the first decade of the 20th century rubber cultivation boomed. By 1930 two thirds of the cultivated land on the Peninsula would be under rubber.

Malayan tin and Malayan rubber would dominate their respective world markets, and, despite their price instability, would make the Peninsula one of Britain's most valued imperial possessions. The success of these commodities meant that economic diversification was limited. Crops such as pepper, sugar and coffee were largely swept aside by rubber after 1900. Some limited progress was made with palm oil, pineapples and timber in the more cautious 1920s and 1930s. No significant industrialisation occurred. However the road and rail networks which the British established formed the basis for a good communications infrastructure. Chinese activity in such areas as finance, transportation, construction, small scale industry and retail trading was also establishing a strong base for the area's economic future.

Chinese immigration swelled in the colonial era, pulled by the economic opportunities opening up and pushed by the dire conditions in China. The British left Chinese immigration uncontrolled until 1930, when the Great Depression ended any demand for additional labour. Meanwhile the British had also recruited Indian labour. The Chinese and Indians had always been regarded as transients, but by the 1930s significant numbers had either decided to settle or lacked the ability to return to their homelands. The 1931 census revealed that Malays no longer formed the majority in the total population of the Malay States and Straits Settlements. This was despite another aspect of immigration to the Peninsula in this era – the arrival in substantial numbers of Malay-Muslim people from various parts of the Archipelago.

Divisions between Malays, Chinese and Indians, already culturally profound, were deepened by British perceptions and policies. Racial stereotyping meant that the Malays were effectively excluded from the modernising economy. Their upper class was encouraged to think about an English public school-style education and a career within the branch of government which administered the Malays. Ordinary Malays were envisaged as rice farmers and fisherfolk, and their vernacular education was tailored to such humble goals.

The growing towns and cities of colonial Malaya, predominantly populated by Chinese, became alien places to most Malays. Meanwhile the Chinese were subject to a separate branch of government and managed their own education systems, in Chinese languages or English. Most Indians were effectively subjects of the rubber estates on which they laboured; their children received Indian language education.

Such separation of the communities made the emergence of nationalism, in the sense of a pan-ethnic movement, unlikely. Prior to World War II the British in Malaya were virtually unbothered by the sort of anti-colonial sentiment disturbing other Western colonies in Asia. Divisions within Malaya's communities furthered this state of affairs. Most Malays still tended to be loyal to their particular state and sultan. The Chinese were divided by differences of clan and dialect, and by the battle between Kuomintang and Communists in China.

However, education in various forms was beginning to produce people within each of the ethnic communities who were not content to leave the future entirely to the British. Amongst Malays, pan-Malay and pan-Muslim attitudes were stirring in the 1930s, heralding strong Malay political organisation later. A few Malay radicals believed that the Peninsula should become part of the Indonesia envisaged by the nationalists of the Netherlands East Indies. The Communist Party of Malaya, founded in 1930, was mainly Chinese in membership and in the 1930s mainly interested in events in China, but it had begun to analyse the potential for revolution in Malaya. Many Indians were gaining political confidence from news about the struggle against the British in the sub-continent. Soon, war would accelerate dramatically the significance of these political awakenings.

Meanwhile Sarawak and British North Borneo were quiet backwaters of the colonial world. Both had experienced major rebellions against the imposition of white authority, but resistance had been largely put down by 1900. Thereafter, change was slow. Neither territory attracted more than minor economic development, and the Brooke government (from 1917 under the third raja, Vyner Brooke) and the Chartered Company always survived on tight budgets. The

Brookes made a virtue of that fact by arguing that they were deliberately protecting their subjects from the evils of modernisation. The provision of education was extremely limited in both territories, much of it being left to Christian missions.

In one regard – that of racial stereotyping – the theory of administration in Sarawak conformed closely to British theory in the Peninsular states. In Brooke eyes Sarawak's Malay-Muslims would provide native administrators, the immigrant Chinese (over 30 per cent of the population by the early 20th century) would drive the commercial economy, while the Dayaks (Ibans) would remain within their traditional culture, except in the matter of head-hunting, for which the administration substituted police and military work. The Chartered Company, by contrast, was relatively relaxed in its dealings with its ethnically diverse population. It welcomed administrative and commercial talent from any group, and allowed complex intercommunal relationships to flourish. The communal rigidities of Sarawak and the Peninsular states did not therefore develop to the same degree in Sabah.

Japanese occupation

Japanese forces attacked British Malaya on 8 December 1941. Singapore, the supreme symbol of British power in Southeast Asia, fell on 15 February 1942. Sarawak and British North Borneo were occupied without a shot. Over three and a half years of Japanese occupation would follow, until British military administrators would return in August/September 1945. The principal results of these years were devastation of the pre-war economy, a much more politicised populace than before, and also a much more divided populace.

The Japanese presented themselves to Malay-Muslims as their patron, respectful of Islam and of Malay culture. They fostered pan-Malay consciousness and gave Malays new opportunities in administration. They also encouraged those young Malay radicals hoping for links with the Indonesian nationalists, though few Peninsular Malays supported them and the idea would not get far. Japanese regard for the Malays was thrown into question in 1943, however, when they handed over the four northern Malay states to Thailand. (These states would be returned to British control in 1945.)

The Chinese were treated by the Japanese as war enemies, often with appalling brutality. Not surprisingly, Chinese formed the majority of the underground resistance forces which developed in the Peninsula and in the Borneo-territories. The Peninsular forces were known as the MPAJA (Malayan Peoples' Anti-Japanese Army), and were to a large degree controlled by members of the CPM (Communist Party of Malaya).

The Indians of Malaya, by contrast, were encouraged by the Japanese to focus their political thoughts on India. Many young Malayan Indians were recruited for service in the Japanese-sponsored but ill-fated INA (Indian National Army).

The post-war period

When the British returned in 1945 they quickly subdued the open intercommunal hostilities which had flared at the war's end. They were aware, however, that there could be no going back to the complacency of pre-war days. Alongside the massive reconstruction of the economy they also set about fundamental administrative reform. In 1946 Sarawak and British North Borneo – the latter particularly badly damaged by war – were acquired from their former owners and finally became the full responsibility of Britain.

On the Peninsula the British introduced a plan for 'Malayan Union', uniting administratively the Malay States, Penang and Melaka (though not Singapore) and giving all residents equal rights of citizenship.

Malays from all states were galvanized by the blithe disregard for states' rights and Malay pre-eminence over the immigrant peoples. UMNO (United Malays National Organisation) was swiftly formed in protest, and the British were forced to abandon the idea of union. In subsequent talks UMNO agreed, however, to a federal administrative structure, and to citizenship for non-Malays who filled certain strict criteria. The Federation of Malaya was launched in 1948.

In the same year the CPM attempted revolution, using guerrilla warfare tactics and drawing on the experience and organisation gained during the war in the MPAJA. The British declared a state of emergency (the event became known as 'the Emergency') and developed counter-insurgency policies which, crucially, won the support of the majority of the population.

By the early 1950s CPM terrorism had been reduced to a minor problem, though emergency regulations were not lifted until 1960. One permanent result of the Emergency was a highly centralised federation, the states having relinquished most of their sovereign powers so that the crisis could be handled efficiently.

Alliance government and Independence

During the Emergency the British promised self-government for Malaya, though at the time it was not clear how this could be achieved in a way acceptable to all communities. Attempts to establish multi-racial political parties met with little success. The largest and best organised party in Malaya, UMNO, was exclusively for Malays. The peril of politicised ethnic rivalry loomed large.

Beginning in 1952, however, a formula for potentially stable self-government was worked out. This was the Alliance, a coalition of three communal based parties. UMNO represented the Malays. The Chinese were represented by the new and politically conservative MCA (Malayan – later Malaysian – Chinese Association). The Malayan – later Malaysian – Indian Congress (MIC) represented the Indian community. The Alliance testified to the pragmatic good sense, diplomatic skills and political generosity of its founders, supremely Tunku Abdul Rahman, UMNO leader and first Prime Minister until 1970. Hugely successful at national elections in 1955, the Alliance achieved merdeka (independence) for the Federation of Malaya in 1957. The new nation's democratic parliamentary system and its legal system were broadly derived from British models.

The Alliance was not without its flaws, leaving unresolved many issues which Malaysia is still working out. It was a pact, or bargain, between three communal élites which gave the economically weak Malays access to political and administrative power while assuring the other communities of respect for their interests. The Malays were offered a degree of 'positive discrimination' but Alliance government basically left the socio-economic imbalances between communities to be worked out by laissez faire forces. In addition, questions of national cultural integration were left largely unresolved. Malay pre-eminence was acknowledged in adopting Islam as the national religion, in the form of monarchy devised (the nine hereditary state rulers would elect a king from their number every five years), and in making Malay the national language, but the application of the national religion and language to the daily lives of non-Malays was extremely circumscribed. It was believed that inter-ethnic suspicions were running too high for such issues to be determined at once.

The creation of Malaysia

Ethnic issues dominated the formation of the Federation of Malaysia. First mooted in 1961, Malaysia was envisaged as a merger of Malaya with Singapore, Sarawak, Sabah (still then British North Borneo) and, perhaps, the sultanate of Brunei. In the event Brunei remained apart, but after cautious negotiation the other territories established Malaysia on 16 September 1963.

The new nation was a delicate exercise in ethnic arithmetic. The non-Chinese majorities of the Borneo states helped balance the inclusion of the predominantly Chinese Singapore, but Singapore entered Malaysia with many constitutional, political and administrative issues left unresolved. Tensions escalated and in August 1965 Tunku Abdul Rahman and Lee Kuan Yew signed a separation agreement.

The 1969 crisis

The 1960s saw Malaysian democracy at its most open, and a number of parties engaging in vigorous criticism of the Alliance. The most notable opposition parties were PAS (Parti Islam Se-Malaysia, originally PMIP, Pan-Malayan Islamic Party), and DAP (Democratic Action Party). PAS was dedicated to building an Islamic state in Malaysia and appealed to Malay voters who saw UMNO as compromised by Western and non-Islamic influences and too ready to bargain with the non-Malays. The DAP picked up support mainly from Chinese voters unhappy with the conservative and Malay-dominated Alliance.

Political passions ran high during the general election campaign of May 1969. The results appeared to diminish the absolute control over government which the Alliance had previously enjoyed. Violent clashes erupted in Kuala Lumpur between perturbed Malays and celebratory Chinese. The riots lasted four days and caused several hundred deaths and heavy destruction of property. A state of emergency was declared and government placed effectively in the hands of a body coordinating military and police action, the National Operations Council (NOC). Some observers feared that Malaysian democracy was dead. This did not prove to be the outcome, but the rage and trauma did lead to substantial political changes.

UMNO and Barisan Nasional government

Government by NOC ended in 1971 and government by federal cabinet, based on parliamentary voting strength, was restored, but the level of political freedom allowed to critics of government policy in the 1960s did not return. Conciliation and consensus-building were to remain a key feature of the Malaysian political scene, but now non-Malays were left in no doubt that their bargaining position was weaker than it may have seemed before May 1969. Malaysian government now adopted much more frankly the character of a primarily Malay government of a primarily Malay nation. Malay interests became paramount in the formulation of government goals and policies. UMNO became unapologetically the dominant political party in Malaysia, and was to increase its power further over the next two decades.

Under Tun Abdul Razak, Prime Minister until his death in 1976, the Alliance was superseded by a broader coalition of parties, Barisan Nasional (popularly 'Barisan'). MCA and MIC remained within this coalition but with their influence diluted. The leading pre-1969 opposition parties, however, refused to be subsumed within the UMNO-dominated coalition. DAP has always remained outside Barisan. Pas joined briefly but soon departed. At the present time Pas controls the state government of Kelantan but has never been able to win many federal seats.

Barisan was to prove a device for strong UMNO-led government. The composition of the coalition has fluctuated during the 1970s and 1980s, as has the extent of its winning margins at elections, but following the 1990 general election the Barisan, comprised of nine parties, held 127 of the 180 seats in the federal lower house. Of the 127 Barisan seats UMNO held 71; no other component party held more than 18. DAP, with 20 seats, led the five opposition parties.

NEP and economic growth

Even more important for the direction of Malaysian politics was the establishment in 1971 of the New Economic Policy (NEP). Tun Razak and the 'second generation' of Malay politicians saw the need to tackle vigorously the economic and social disparities which fuelled racial antagonism. The NEP set two basic goals with a 1990 target date – to reduce and eventually eradicate poverty, and to reduce and eventually eradicate identification of economic function with race. These goals were to be achieved in the context of high economic growth rates over the next two decades; while NEP would be socially redistributive there would be no absolute 'losers'.

To meet NEP goals, however, NEP would inevitably mean government favour for the Malays, by far the largest component of Malaysia's Bumiputera peoples. In the early 1970s Bumiputeras were still predominantly rural-based and involved in agriculture. Around half of Bumiputera households existed below the poverty line. Bumiputeras owned a mere 1.5 per cent of the share capital of companies operating in Malaysia, and accounted for only 4.9 per cent of the country's registered professionals.

NEP necessitated a dramatic increase in governmental intervention in Malaysian business and in Malaysian society in general. NEP's 'big government' strategies vastly increased UMNO's power and influence. Under NEP the volumes of public investment and public consumption expenditure increased substantially. In order to increase the Bumiputera stake in the economy, major public enterprises were established to take up share capital 'in trust' for Bumiputeras until they were in a position to purchase share capital privately. Some of these enterprises developed elaborate conglomerate business interests.

Government promoted the education and training of Bumiputeras, and access for them at all levels of the public and private sectors. Government also promoted the modernisation of the rural economy, with its predominantly Bumiputera workforce, and of rural life in general, while also supervising the balanced expansion of urban areas. In general, NEP saw the creation of significant Bumiputera commercial, industrial and professional communities. The percentage of Bumiputera households in Peninsular Malaysia deemed in poverty dropped by 1987 to 17.3 per cent in rural areas and about 8 per cent in urban areas.

Simultaneously with the implementation of NEP the Malaysian economy experienced dramatic growth. In the years 1971–1990 the country's annual average growth in GNP was 6.8 per cent. Per capita GDP moved from $380 to $2,200 (in current US$). Once the purveyor of just two important commodities, rubber and tin, Malaysia now also became a major exporter of oil/LNG, palm oil, timber and manufactures. Growth in manufacturing was particularly spectacular.

By the late 1980s manufactures dominated Malaysia's exports. Major manufactures included electrical and electronic products, chemicals, processed foods, textiles and processed timber and rubber products. Steel and automobile industries had also been established. The opening of new economic opportunities and the solid rise in prosperity helped mollify those non-Bumiputeras who had feared NEP and who still disliked many of its features, notably the level of government control over business and the favouritism shown towards Malays in areas such as education and employment.

Critics of NEP also argued that its implementation had paid insufficient attention to the non-Malay Bumiputera communities of Sarawak and Sabah, which are now the states with the worst figures on poverty in Malaysia. In 1987 the percentage of Bumiputera households deemed in poverty in Sarawak was 33 per cent; the percentage for Sabah was almost 42 per cent. The critics also argued that the Chinese and Indian poor had been ignored, and that even within the Malay community NEP benefits had tended to be spread to UMNO's political advantage rather than on the basis of equity.

Eventually economic pressures compelled modification of NEP's 'big government' strategies. In the mid 1980s a drastic fall in commodity prices, virtually across the board, threatened a serious balance of payments crisis. Datuk Seri Dr Mahathir Mohamad, Prime Minister since 1981, and his then Finance Minister Daim Zainuddin pegged back government spending and instituted a policy of privatisation of public enterprises.

Mahathir, a strident champion of Malay advancement, was also motivated to modify NEP strategies by his fear that Malay 'feather bedding' would prove self-defeating. NEP has now been replaced by NDP (New Development Policy) which, though retaining NEP's broad goals, aims in Dr Mahathir's words to 'strike an optimum balance between the goals of economic growth and equity'. It is claimed that NDP strategies will concentrate on the more glaring pockets of poverty and disadvantage still existing in a now relatively prosperous Malaysia.

Mahathir and the centralisation of power

Dr Mahathir has been a controversial figure. Before achieving the Prime Ministership in 1981 he was often viewed as a Malay radical who might exacerbate Malaysia's ethnic tensions. In power, however, he has proved a more complex political personality.

Mahathir has championed the Malays yet he lambasts the dependent attitudes which he thinks NEP fostered. He has promoted Islam in Malaysia, yet reined in its more doctrinaire elements and sharply rebuked Islamic 'fanaticism'. He has insisted on the political overlordship of UMNO more forcefully than any previous administration, yet made it clear that non-Malays may work within the Barisan system securely and profitably. Mahathir will go to the brink in pursuit of his political goals, yet he has never actually plunged Malaysia into any of the impasses, ethnic or cultural, of which it could be capable.

Even so, there is a clear theme to Mahathir's Prime Ministership – the centralisation of all significant power in the hands of the person who jointly heads UMNO and, as Prime Minister, the national government. Mahathir would argue that such concentration of power is necessary for social stability and economic development. Critics argue that he has unnecessarily diminished the democratic freedoms which Malaysia – unusually in its region – enjoyed. They also claim that the growth of government power has led to the abuse of power. Barisan government is continually dogged with rumours of corruption, though the rumours remain unproven.

Ironically, Mahathir's major battles for control have concerned divisions within the Malay community, not inter-communal divisions. The opposition party DAP now commands a majority of Chinese votes but politically it is impotent except as a persistent but cautiously phrased critic of government. Mahathir's biggest political challenge occurred in 1986–87 when elements of his own party UMNO rebelled against his leadership. Partly this was a matter of personalities and of discontent with Mahathir's dominating style, but the revolt also signalled Malay alarm at the administration's retreat from NEP's 'big government' strategies. Mahathir retained the UMNO presidency by a mere 43 vote margin over his rival Tunku Razaleigh Hamzah (the voting was 761–718). After his victory Mahathir purged his cabinet. Razaleigh subsequently established a rival party for Malays, Semangat 46.

Political tension persisted and in October 1987 Mahathir clamped down, detaining 106 people including leading opposition personalities. Three newspapers were closed including the Star which carried a column by the first Prime Minister Tunku Abdul Rahman (who has since died) often critical of Mahathir government. Most of the detainees were released within weeks, Mahathir's drastic action having subdued much of the political agitation.

Elements of the judiciary questioned the legal extent of the government's powers of detention without trial. The detentions had been ordered under the ISA (Internal Security Act), a measure created by the British in Emergency days and originally intended for use against communists. In recent years the ISA has been used frequently to muffle debate when political feelings run high.

In response to the judiciary's concerns many feel Mahathir arranged the suspension of the head of the judiciary, Mohamed Salleh Abbas, and subsequently the suspension of five of the Supreme Court judges listed to hear Salleh's appeal against his suspension. Ever since, the Malaysian Bar Council has maintained a 'boycott' against the succeeding judiciary head, in protest at the perceived subordination of the law to the executive.

At the 1990 general election the breakaway Semangat 46 established links with DAP, PAS and other opposition parties, claiming that they were offering voters a credible alternative coalition government. In broad terms, however, the voters stayed with the status quo, doubting the opposition parties' capacity to maintain stability. The opposition parties also suffered in the face of Barisan's vastly superior financial resources and near monopoly of media information. Since his 1990 victory Mahathir has reigned securely, and political analysts expect him to carry elections for the foreseeable future. Other areas in which Mahathir has insisted on imposing his power include the promotion of Islam in Malaysia, the powers of Malaysian royalty, centre-state relationships, and UMNO's choice of a potential successor.

From the 1960s Malaysian government has had to deal with increased levels of Muslim political assertiveness. The traditionally quiet religious culture of the Malays has been shaken by the dakwah (mission) movement and by the claims of the opposition party PAS that UMNO is insufficiently concerned with religious matters. The dual thrust of the dakwah movement has been to foster personal devoutness and to pressure Malaysian government to support a more Islamic society. The movement has been particularly identified with young, educated and politically aware Malays.

In response, Barisan government has demonstrated strong support for Islam in a range of ways. With government patronage Malaysia today is a much more insistently Islamic society than it was. But government activity in this area has also had a restraining dimension, aiming to bring Islamic enthusiasms under government oversight and regulation. During the 1980s several legislative measures tightened government powers over religious organisations and their teaching. On occasion the government has resorted to its tough detention and censorship powers to silence persons considered a threat to social order on religious grounds. As well, government has used all its political skills and media control to diminish the credibility of PAS in Malay eyes. However PAS survives strongly in the northeastern Peninsular states of Kelantan and Trengganu and can score around 20 per cent of the vote in national elections.

The government has also removed the powers of the Malaysian king to veto legislation, and minimised royal power to delay legislation. He has also cut the powers and privileges of the country's nine royal state rulers, following an orchestrated media campaign in 1993 which alleged the contempt of some rulers for the law, their questionable business dealings and extravagant lifestyles. Once held up as the symbols of historic Malay culture the rulers were pilloried as 'feudal relics', at odds with the contemporary business and technology-oriented Malay. The Malaysian Bar Council's view was that the executive's reduction of the rulers' powers was a further attack on constitutional democracy in Malaysia.

Mahathir has always given frank expression to his hostility towards Malaysian states which defy Barisan government and elect opposition state governments. Kelantan is currently the object of his displeasure for its Pas-controlled government. In March 1994 Mahathir scored a victory, however, when

Barisan dislodged from government in Sabah the opposition United Sabah Party (PBS).

In contrast to Sarawak, which since the 1960s has experienced Alliance/Barisan government under Malay leadership, Sabah has had difficulty in conforming to national political norms. Multiracial Sabah has tended to reject attempts to divide it politically along communal lines, and also resented federal domination of its affairs. PBS is led and basically supported by the mainly Christian Kadazan-Dusun peoples of Sabah (around 40 per cent of the state's population) but has appealed to many voters from other communities. In 1991 UMNO established a branch in Sabah and set about organising a Barisan-style coalition of parties opposed to PBS. In the March 1994 election PBS won a two-seat majority, but was subsequently forced to give up its claim to government when several PBS members were induced to defect to Barisan. Once again UMNO's financial resources and political clout carried the day.

Mahathir will only turn 70 in 1995, and looks set to establish a record term for a Malaysian prime minister. UMNO has been considering the succession nevertheless, precipitating sharp competition between possible candidates, but at party elections in late 1993 Mahathir's preferred choice of heir, Finance Minister Datuk Seri Anwar Ibrahim, easily carried the day.

TIMELINES

1990: Elections declared null and void by SLORC

1988: State Law and Order Restoration Council (SLORC) assumes control under General Saw Maung. Union of Myanmar formed

1974: New Constitution and formation of Socialist Republic of the Union of Burma

1962: Military coup led by General Ne Win ushers in 'Burmese Way to Socialism'

1948-62: Period of democratic governments

1948: Independence granted and the Union of Burma formed

1886: Britain annexes what is left of Myanmar

1824-26 & 1850s: First and Second Anglo-Burmese Wars result in the loss of territory to the British East India Company

mid 18th century: New kingdom emerges at Ava (near Mandalay)

mid 16th century: New kingdom emerges at Pegu (near Rangoon)

end 13 century: Mongols from China attack Pagan and empire is destroyed

1044: Pagan empire founded

ASEAN FOCUS GROUP

Myanmar

Myanmar, formerly known as Burma, is a unique country in Southeast Asia. For most of the five decades since achieving independence in the aftermath of the second world war, Myanmar has isolated itself from the outside world. From its pre-war position as a relatively rich agricultural colony and a major exporter of rice it has slumped to being the poorest nation in Southeast Asia. Mineral rich, in the 1990s it is dependent on oil imports to keep its economy running. Ruled by a military regime since 1962, for more than thirty years it deliberately isolated itself from the political, social and economic forces that have swept over the rest of Southeast Asia in the past three decades. However, in the mid 1990s there are signs that economic imperatives and political pressure from both inside and outside the country are leading to more outward looking economic policies.

Myanmar is the most ethnically diverse state in mainland Southeast Asia. The Burmese comprise around 68 per cent of the population, but there are more than one hundred ethnic groups in the country. The Burmese dominate the alluvial plains and the major towns and cities. The hills bordering the neighbouring countries of India, Bangladesh, China, Laos and Thailand are populated by ethnic minorities. These peoples have long resisted Burmese domination. The largest of the ethnic minorities are the Shans, the Karens and the Arakanese. The multi-ethnic nature of Myanmar and the antipathy by the ethnic minorities towards Burmese domination is one important theme in Myanmar's history.

The Burmese are predominantly Buddhist, whereas the Karen and the Shan are predominantly Christian and the Arakanese are split between Buddhists and Muslims. Buddhism entered Myanmar from India from the seventh century and along with it came Hindu-Buddhist cosmological ideas. The ethnic Burmese began their migration from southern China in the ninth century and over the succeeding thousand years steadily spread through the lowland plains of present-day Myanmar. The Burmese embraced Buddhism. Christianity was introduced during British rule, with British missionaries evangelising among the animistic hill peoples, converting the Shan, Karen and other ethnic minorities to the Christian faith. The coincidence of ethnicity and religion has deepened the divisions between ethnic groups in Myanmar.

A second major theme in Myanmar's history is a deep concern about its neighbours. The Burmese and the Thais have competed for territory, power and wealth over hundreds of years, resorting to war where necessary and thoroughly distrusting each other in periods of peace. The Burmese have also ingrained fears of their huge northern neighbour China (remembering the Mongol conquest at the end of the thirteenth century) and still fresh memories of Indian migrants during the colonial period, who dominated the modern sector of the economy.

Pre-colonial history

The territorial boundaries of Myanmar are the creation of British colonialism. Prior to British conquest no indigenous kingdom controlled the territory that now makes up Myanmar. The division between the alluvial plains (the lowlands) and the mountainous regions (the highlands) is central not just to the history of Myanmar but to the history of all mainland Southeast Asian states. Lowland Myanmar is dominated by the Irrawaddy river and the rich alluvial plain was created and re-created by thousands of years of annual monsoonal flooding.

The first known kingdoms emerged in the lower Irrawaddy valley from the 5th century. They were non-Burmese kingdoms but strongly influenced by Hindu-Buddhism ideas. The first major kingdom was founded around 1044, on the banks of the Irrawaddy river at Pagan (now known as Bagan), north of the present day capital of Yangon (formerly known as Rangoon). For over two hundred years, until the end of the 13th century, the Pagan empire flourished, at its peak controlling much of the territory of present-day Myanmar. It was a Buddhist kingdom whose temple remains at Pagan attest not only to its great agricultural wealth but also to its people's knowledge of mathematics, geometry and engineering. The temples of Pagan stretch along a forty square kilometre zone on the banks of the Irrawaddy river. Some are as large as medieval European cathedrals, though built a century or more earlier. Pagan remains a golden era in the Burmese mind, when a strong, prosperous Burmese kingdom created beautiful temples and religiously inspired works of arts, and was a renowned centre for Buddhist scholarship.

The first major Burmese kingdom was destroyed by a northern invader when Pagan was attacked by the Mongols from China at the end of the 13th century. The city of Pagan itself was sacked and subsequently abandoned. Only the temples remained, under the control of Buddhist monasteries. In its place for the next three hundred years were a series of small competing rulers all of whom failed to re-create the glories of Pagan. In the middle of the 16th century a new Burmese kingdom emerged at Pegu, near Rangoon, and tried to reunite the Burmese. It quickly exerted control over much of lower Myanmar and north to the Shan states. But it was a short-lived state, collapsing after only fifty years. Once again the Burmese were divided by a number of small, competing kingdoms.

In the middle of the 18th century a new Burmese kingdom emerged at Ava (near Mandalay). It gradually extended its control over much of what is now Myanmar, including conquering the hill states of the Shan people. It became a major regional power, competing with the Thai kingdom of Ayudhya for territory and people. The Thai/Burmese rivalry was strong and often bitter. In 1767 Ava was strong enough to despatch an army to the Thai capital of Ayudhya. The capital was sacked, treasures were looted (with many finding a home today in

Burmese museums), and tens of thousands of Thais captured and transported back to Myanmar as slaves. The Thai kingdom collapsed, to be replaced a few years later by a new kingdom, the Chakri dynasty, which continues today in Thailand and whose capital was built further south at Bangkok away from the threat of Burmese attack.

At the end of the 18th century Myanmar was the strongest state in mainland Southeast Asia. The Chakri dynasty in Thailand was in its infancy, recovering from the Burmese destruction of Ayudhya, and the Vietnamese kingdom was torn by rebellion. The balance changed in the early nineteenth century: the Thai and Vietnamese kingdoms flourished while the Burmese kingdom declined. The Burmese ruling elite was noticeably more inward-looking than its Thai and Vietnamese counterparts and less involved in commercial relations with the outside world. As Britain increased its presence in Southeast Asia in the 19th century the Burmese elite proved less able than the Thais to appreciate the threat posed to them and therefore less able to adopt strategies to cope with them.

The colonial period

The British East India Company (EIC) steadily extended its territory in India from early in the 17th century. Bengal, on the east coast of India adjacent to the Burmese kingdom of Ava, was the British stepping stone into India. Calcutta was the capital from which emanated EIC influence, territorial expansion and commercial dealings. Myanmar was primarily seen by the EIC as a buffer zone. It had potential commercial importance but its greater importance was strategic. No other European power could be allowed to gain influence there and the Burmese rulers were expected to acknowledge the superiority of British India and create stable conditions for successful trade.

The Burmese king and elite had a very different view of the world and the Burmese place in it. Fresh from conquering Ayudhya, in the 1820s the Burmese kingdom extended its control over Arakan, bordering Bengal. Refugees fled across the border from where they organised resistance to the Burmese. The Burmese king finally demanded the British return them. For their part, the British became increasingly concerned about political instability on their colonial frontier.

The Burmese court greatly underestimated the strength of the EIC. In 1822 Burmese forces invaded Bengal and threatened to march on Chittagong in a dispute over the return of political refugees from Ava. The result was a British expedition to Myanmar. The Burmese were no easy opponents. The first Anglo–Burmese war lasted two years, from 1824 until 1826. Eventually superior British weaponry and tactics, backed by a strong rear base in Bengal, ensured a British victory. The Burmese were forced to cede a large amount of territory on the coast of the Bay of Bengal. The EIC now controlled the Bay of Bengal from both sides. Over the next two decades the EIC exploited the agricultural potential of its new territory, increasing rice production four-fold and developing a strong export trade in rice, timber and shipbuilding.

Despite this defeat and loss of territory, the Burmese elite still underestimated British power in Bengal, demanding respect as equals and taking whatever opportunities they could to remind British envoys, traders and visitors of their equal status. In the 1850s a second Anglo–Burmese war broke out, the immediate cause of which was a conflict between British traders and the Burmese governor of Rangoon. The result was that Bengal acquired more territory in lower Myanmar. The final act in the British acquisition of Myanmar occurred in 1885 when Mandalay was captured and the King and his family exiled to Calcutta. Myanmar was formally annexed by Britain on 1 January 1886.

The British impact on Myanmar was profound. At the political level the monarchy was abolished and the Burmese aristocracy were stripped of their power. Myanmar was ruled from Calcutta, as a minor part of the British Indian empire. Indian models of administration were imposed by the British who, by and large, had no understanding of or respect for local social structures. Lower Myanmar, that is the alluvial plains which were ethnically Burmese and the heart of the Burmese empires, was ruled directly by the colonial government with the powers of traditional regional and local elites destroyed. It was here that the full force of British political and economic policies were felt.

In Upland Myanmar, in areas populated by ethnic groups such as the Shan and Karen, a policy of indirect rule was introduced. Social structures and local elites were more or less left intact with administrations separate from that of the Burmese heartland. A major consequence was to strengthen the division between the Burmese and ethnic minorities, with the latter developing a stronger sense of identity under British rule.

It has been argued that one of the most important consequences of British conquest was that the two most vital institutions of Burmese society, which together defined what it meant to be Burmese, were destroyed or seriously weakened. The exile of the king and his family meant that the ritual and symbolism of the Court was abruptly ended. The Burmese state no longer had a centre, indeed the throne itself was transported to a museum in Calcutta. The king was also the patron and in many senses the head of the Buddhist hierarchy. His demise reduced the authority of the religious hierarchy, leaving Buddhist religious institutions with a much weakened central leadership. As a consequence they fragmented. These two binding forces in Burmese society were eliminated with no indigenous replacements.

British colonial rule introduced a strong bureaucracy supported in its maintenance of social control by an efficient police and army. The British distrusted the Burmese. The police and the army were largely composed of ethnic minorities who would have few qualms about quashing Burmese dissent. The bureaucracy was British supervised but staffed largely by Anglo–Burmese and Indians. The new bureaucratic elite created by Britain was dominated by Anglo–Burmese, whose cultural models were influenced more by Britain than by Myanmar. This was to pose considerable problems after independence.

British rule increased the ethnic diversity of Myanmar. The administrative link with India meant that Indians were free to migrate. By 1931, about 7 per cent of the population of Myanmar was Indian, predominantly from Bengal and Madras. Yangon was an immigrant city. Two-thirds of its population in 1931 were immigrants, including 53 per cent Indians. Much of the capital for the agricultural expansion in the Myanmar Delta came from Indian moneylenders. Chinese immigrants were recruited from British Malaya and Singapore. In 1931, they composed about 2 per cent of the total population of Myanmar. They worked in the mines in the Shan states, provided much of the urban labour force, operated small businesses and built rice mills in central Myanmar. On the eve of British conquest the Myanmar lowlands were populated predominantly by ethnic Burmese. By 1941, this ethnic homogeneity had given way to a multi-ethnic, multi-religious society.

The British transformed Myanmar's economy. They encouraged the settlement of the Myanmar Delta, largely malarial infested jungle and swamps, in the 1850s. Roads and bridges were built, land was opened up at cheap prices with significant tax concessions and the infrastructure of ports and communications was greatly improved to enable crops to be exported to world markets. The result was a dramatic southward migration of Burmese from the dry northern zone to the fertile delta.

The Myanmar Delta became a major producer of rice and little else, commercialised and dependent on the vagaries of international markets. The extent of the transformation can be gauged by the raw economic statistics. In 1855 lower Myanmar exported 162,000 tons of rice: in 1905–6 it exported two million tons, with the price of rice increasing threefold in that time. The area under rice cultivation expanded from around 800,000 acres to around 6 million acres and the population grew from one million in 1852 to four million in 1901.

Land was plentiful until the 1920s when the limits of cultivation were reached. Until then the Myanmar Delta was generally prosperous, for those who tilled the land as well as for those who financed the development and traded rice and teak on world markets. From the 1920s population pressure on the land became a major problem, as did farmer indebtedness. Tensions between Burmese and immigrant Chinese and Indians then became more open and at times more violent.

Britain was content for Myanmar to be a rice, teak and mineral exporter and there was no attempt to industrialise. In 1941 Myanmar was still a relatively prosperous agrarian society, though serious indebtedness and population pressure had expressed themselves in peasant protests and violence in the 1930s. What capitalism existed was in foreign hands: European companies controlled the export trade, the petty traders and small scale capitalists were Chinese and the financiers and rural moneylenders were Indians. Myanmar was a plural society in which economic position was coterminous with ethnicity.

Economic development under colonial rule was accompanied by the spread of western education. A new western-educated, urban elite emerged in the 20th century out of which came a nationalist movement. As part of the Indian empire, until its separation into an independent colony in 1937, Myanmar's political development closely paralleled that of India. The political reforms introduced in India from the beginning of the 20th century were extended to Myanmar. In 1935 a new Constitution was introduced into Myanmar under which limited self-government was permitted. The first elections for a Burmese Parliament were held in 1936 and a Westminster-style parliamentary government operated until the Japanese occupation in 1942.

The nationalist movement in Myanmar had a number of distinctive characteristics. First, it was dominated by the ethnic Burmese. Their promotion of Burmese language, literature and cultural symbols as 'national', led to an ambiguous relationship with the ethnic minorities who were suspicious of the nationalist movement. They feared Burmese domination of an independent Myanmar and their assimilation into Burmese majority culture. Second, the nationalist movement was strongly anti-Chinese and anti-Indian, in reaction to these groups' domination of the economy. Third, the domination of the Myanmar economy by foreign capital stimulated the development of socialist ideology among all strands of Burmese nationalism. Fourth, the stress on Buddhism as being at the core of Burmans' cultural, religious and personal identity further alienated the non-Burmese minorities, especially those who were Christians.

On the eve of the Second World War there was a strong urban based, western-educated nationalist elite which had developed no single or widely accepted view of what independent Myanmar would look like, apart from a stress on the unity of Myanmar, the Burmeseness of Myanmar and the need to take control of the economy out of the hands of foreigners. Two of the most prominent nationalists in the 1930s were Aung San (father of Aung San Suu Kyi) and U Nu, the latter of whom was to be the first Prime Minister and who died in his 80s in early 1995. Another member was Ne Win, who in 1962 led the coup that placed the military in power, where they remain in the 1990s. Japan became a magnet for many nationalists in the 1930s. They were impressed by its propaganda support of anti-colonial movements in Southeast Asia. When the Second World War broke out Aung San was one of a group known as the Thirty Comrades who accepted Japanese-sponsored military training in Hainan. The Thirty Comrades returned to Myanmar in 1942 along with the invading Japanese army as leaders of the Myanmar Independence Army. From the Thirty Comrades came many of the political and military leaders of post-independent Myanmar.

Japanese Occupation

The Japanese occupation was welcomed by many Burmese, including, of course, the Thirty Comrades. The attraction of Japan in the 1930s was shared by most Southeast Asian nationalists. Not only did the Japanese decisively end European colonialism but their slogans of 'Asia for the Asians' and building a 'Co-Prosperity Sphere' were seductive. The destruction of white rule was itself a major fillip to Southeast Asian nationalists. The introduction of military training, the promotion of locals to administrative positions far higher than they could achieve under colonial rule and the promotion of indigenous languages all contributed to a growing self confidence among nationalists throughout the region.

The realities of the Japanese exercise of power were far different from the promises held out by the propaganda. Southeast Asians quickly found Japanese rule to be no less exploitative and far more brutal than that of their former European colonial masters. In 1944, Aung San and fellow members of the Thirty Comrades group established the Anti-Fascist People's Freedom League which opposed the Japanese and worked to develop a vision of an independent Myanmar.

Independence

The activities of the Anti-Fascist People's Freedom League against the Japanese made its leader Aung San a Burmese hero and ensured that at the end of the war Britain would have to negotiate with them. In May 1945, just two weeks after Yangon had been reconquered, Britain announced its plans for post-war Myanmar. Its stated intention was to move Myanmar towards full self-government within the British Commonwealth, but in the meantime to suspend the political reforms of the 1930s and rule directly in order to reconstruct the economy. The plan had no timetable for independence.

Britain's position was unrealistic. It took no account of the political and psychological impact of the Japanese occupation of Southeast Asia. Southeast Asians were no longer prepared to acquiesce in colonial rule. In Myanmar, the Anti-Fascist People's Freedom League, the Burmese Communist Party and parties based on ethnic minorities campaigned for independence and struggled with each other for dominance. In January 1947 Aung San led an Anti-Fascist People's Freedom League delegation to London and negotiated the election of a constituent assembly to prepare a constitution for an independent Myanmar. In April 1947 the Anti-Fascist People's Freedom League won the election handsomely, but in July Aung San and six of his Cabinet were assassinated by political rivals. The assassinations created a national martyr but made it even more difficult for Myanmar to create a consensus on the structure of the independent State.

Aung San was replaced by his deputy U Nu and the Anti-Fascist People's Freedom League led Myanmar into independence on 4 January 1948. The Union of Burma was constituted as a federal state composed of the large Burmese area and four upland states, home to the ethnic minorities. These states were promised a great deal of autonomy. In practice, power over the states was quickly concentrated in the central government. The failure of the federal system and the concentration of power in Yangon has been a major cause of the instability Myanmar has suffered since 1948.

Shortly after independence was declared the Burmese Communist Party and the Karen nationalist movement launched insurrections. The insurrections continue through to the 1990s, though in recent years there have been some conciliatory moves by Yangon to accommodate the rebels and the scale of the fighting has, temporarily, been reduced. The cause of the insurrections remains. Many of the minorities see independent Myanmar as a Burmese state. The army, the police and the apparatus of government are controlled by Burmese. The substantial ethnic minorities fear absorption and the consequent disappearance of their separate and distinct cultural identities.

Myanmar was a democratic state between 1948 and 1962. Governments were elected, accepted the need to operate within the limits of the Constitution, held national elections and abided by the results and accepted decisions of the Supreme Court when it ruled against the government. Power was in the hands of the Anti-Fascist People's Freedom League which drew on the name of Aung San to bolster its support. There was a sixteen month period of military rule between 1958 and 1960, but General Ne Win abided by the Constitution and fulfilled an undertaking to hold elections in 1960. The political party favoured by the military did not win the elections but the military accepted the decision and returned to barracks.

The failings of the democratic period were critical. The declining economy and the stress on the Burmeseness of Myanmar were the prime causes of regional insurrections and social unrest in both urban and rural areas. All efforts to create a social consensus on the kind of society that should be created failed. Corruption became rampant as inflation remorselessly ate away at civil servants' salaries, forcing them to resort to illegal impositions in order to survive.

In March 1962 a military coup led by General Ne Win overthrew the elected government of U Nu. It ushered in a period of military rule that has lasted for over thirty years. The ostensible reason for the coup was the military's fear that Prime Minister U Nu's government would allow the Shan and other ethnic minorities to secede from Myanmar. Many Burmese cautiously welcomed the coup because it promised to put an end to the corruption, instability, inflation and social unrest of the previous decade and a half.

The coup leaders arrested political and ethnic minority leaders, closed down the parliament and demolished the federal structure. Opposition from Yangon students and from Burmese monks was ruthlessly suppressed. The country was ruled by a Revolutionary Council composed entirely of military officials loyal to General Ne Win. The military created its own political party, the Burma Socialist Program Party, as the only legal party in the country and described its ideology as the 'Burmese Way to Socialism'.

In 1974 a new Constitution was put into practice, creating the Socialist Republic of the Union of Burma. An elected parliament was formed, but only one candidate was allowed to stand for each constituency and that candidate had to be approved by the Burma Socialist Program Party.

The military officers who overthrew the elected government in 1962 argued that in the existing chaos the army was the only cohesive and disciplined organisation in society able to provide the strong leadership needed. It was fiercely anti-foreign and determined to rid Myanmar of all vestiges of colonialism by refocussing on Burmese culture, language, tradition and religion.

Like the royal elite that had ruled Myanmar in the 1800s, it was (although this now appears to be changing) an inward looking elite, suspicious of its immediate neighbours and determined to keep outside political, cultural and economic influences to a minimum. It moved quickly to eliminate the business class, because it was predominantly Indian and Chinese, seeing state socialism as the only way to deliver economic independence to the country.

The westernised, often Anglo–Burmese, elite that had run the country under colonial rule and through the 1950s fled the country, along with the Indian and Chinese communities. In the early 1990s they were followed by the Muslim minority on the western border with Bangladesh who too became a target for a Burmese government intent on removing all non-Burmese elements from society.

Ne Win's military government was even less successful than the democratically elected governments before it in developing the Burmese economy. Indeed, the economy worsened acutely under military rule, with the expulsion of Indians and Pakistanis, the prohibition on foreign investment and the efforts of the one-party State to impose a command economy. In 1987 the United Nations gave Myanmar 'Least Developed Nation' status, recognising it as one of the world's ten poorest countries with a per capita income of no more than US$200. There were, however, two Burmese economies: a legal, largely state controlled economy and a black market economy.

It has been estimated that in the late 1980s illegal trade in Myanmar was three times the official trade, and that the total, non-drug, illegal trade made up about forty per cent of GNP, or about US$3 billion annually. The illegal trade filters through Myanmar's porous borders with China, Thailand, Bangladesh and India. The illegal drug trade would add considerably to the black market figures as the Golden Triangle, centred on Myanmar, is the world's major opium producer. The black market has been crucial to Myanmar's economic survival.

There were sporadic student protests and riots in the 1970s, but these were quelled by the military. A new series of protests began early in 1988, led by students and Buddhist monks. The usual tough reaction from the military this time failed to stop the riots growing in intensity. In August and September 1988 they culminated in widespread strikes and massive demonstrations in the urban areas, coalescing into a demand for an end to military rule. The army reacted, killing thousands of protesters. The horrors of these acts were relayed daily to the television screens throughout the world, eliciting widespread international protests. A new organisation, the State Law and Order Restoration Council (SLORC) took over government under the control of the army chief of staff, General Saw Maung. Nevertheless, Ne Win, who had resigned as chairman of the Burmese Socialist Program Party in August 1988, was thought by many to be the real power behind General Saw Maung.

SLORC decided to hold elections in 1990, presumably because it was concerned at the strong international reaction to the repression of August and September 1988 and it thought it could influence the results of the election. The election campaign did not go as planned. Aung San Suu Kyi, daughter of the revered national martyr Aung San, returned from London and quickly became the major spokesperson for the National League for Democracy (NLD). The NLD campaigned vigorously in 1989, drawing large crowds to its meetings despite the restrictions placed by the government.

Aung San Suu Kyi was a powerful orator and magnetic public figure able to draw on the aura surrounding her father's name. In July 1989 she was placed under house arrest and thousands of NLD supporters, students and other political activists were arrested.

Despite the tough military line the NLD won over three-quarters of the seats when the elections were eventually held in May 1990. The re-named Burmese Socialist Program Party – now the National Union Party – won only 10 seats. SLORC responded by arresting NLD leaders and declaring the election null and void. The military subsequently stated that they would retain power. Aung San Suu Kyi, in early 1995, remains under house arrest, refusing the military government's offer of freedom in return for leaving the country. In October 1991 she was awarded the Nobel Peace prize.

The military seems determined to retain political power. Discussions on a possible new Constitution are focussed on legitimising a powerful place for the military while at the same time responding to international criticism of treatment of opponents. The first steps towards some form of reconciliation between the SLORC and Ang San Suu Kyi were taken in mid 1994 although, at the time of publication of this book in mid 1995, she remains under house arrest without an end in sight.

Myanmar's history continues to haunt it and a stable and prosperous future will, to a large extent, depend upon establishing a political system which skillfully handles the aspirations of the various ethnic groups.

TIMELINES

1992: Ramos elected President

1986: Marcos flees after army leaders support Cory Aquino who had won a snap election

1983: Benigno Aquino assassinated

1972: President Marcos declares Martial Law

1946-72: Period of constitutional democracy similar to the United States

1946: Independence granted

1901: Agreement reached with United States establishing colonial rule

1870s: Nationalist movement born

1565: Spanish settlement on Cebu, moves headquarters to Manila in 1571

mid 16th century: Islam established in Mindanao and slowly spread north

16th century: Sparsely populated Islands that were kinship and village based

Philippines

In 1967 the Philippines joined Indonesia, Malaysia, Thailand and Singapore to form the Association of South East Asian countries – ASEAN. At the time, the Philippines was seen by many as a model of what its partners in ASEAN might become. It had a strong economy, a well educated English-speaking workforce, strong technical and managerial classes and an apparently thriving industrial sector. Within the Southeast Asian region it was favoured by foreign investors. Moreover, it was a parliamentary democracy with a vigorous press and a strong civil society, again pointing to what the rest of ASEAN might become. In 1994, just two and a half decades later, the Philippines economy has only slowly restarted after nearly a decade of regression. The Philippines has been left behind by its ASEAN neighbours. It now has a lower per capita income and has been shunned by foreign investors who have poured money into other countries in the region. For more than ten years the Philippines has experienced enormous social and political instability, including a civil war in the south and private armies almost everywhere else. If one characteristic of contemporary ASEAN countries is the presence of a strong state and a weak civil society then the Philippines is the major exception. It has a weak state and a fragmented society.

The Philippines is different from the rest of Southeast Asia in other ways. It shares with Indonesia and Malaysia a Malay ethnic base, its underlying animistic beliefs share much in common with other countries in the region and it has for many centuries been part of regional trading networks, albeit in a minor way. Yet unique among Southeast Asian countries it was unaffected by Hinduism or Buddhism. The Philippines today is a predominantly Christian country, with around 80% of the population being Catholic. The Spanish colonisers probably prevented the conversion of the islands to Islam, and only the southern islands of Mindanao and the Sulu archipelago are Islamic. In another way it is also unique. The absence of Hindu and Buddhist influences meant that sophisticated concepts of the State and cosmologies which linked the temporal and the spiritual realms were lacking in the pre-colonial Philippines. There were no pre-colonial state structures, socially integrating ideologies or 'great traditions'.

One important consequence is that contemporary Filipinos lack a concrete pre-colonial history from which they can draw inspiration and create national myths. There is nothing in the Philippines' past remotely comparable to the 'golden eras' of Angkor in Cambodia, Pagan in Burma or Majapahit in Indonesia. There is only a pattern of regionalism under the control of local trading families and kinship networks.

Early History

We know little about the political, social or economic structures of the islands now known as the Philippines before the arrival of the Spanish in the mid-16th century. The islands were sparsely populated with largely kinship and village based political organisation. There were well established trading networks between the islands and linking the islands into wider regional networks in Southeast Asia and beyond to China and India. There were also some relatively large entrepots, exchanging local products, ranging from exotic foods to gold, for Chinese pottery, silk and other wares.

Islam was the first of the world religions to impact upon the folk religious base of the peoples of the Philippines. It is impossible to date precisely the arrival of Islam in the southern islands of the Philippines, but we do know that Aceh on the northern tip of Sumatra converted to Islam in the middle of the 14th century and that when Melaka was closed to Muslim traders as a consequence of the Portuguese conquest in 1511 the process of Islamisation in the Indonesian archipelago quickened. The ruler of the northern Borneo state of Brunei converted to Islam soon after the fall of Melaka to the Portuguese. Brunei then became the base for the spread of Islam into the southern islands of the Philippines. By the middle of the 16th century the ruler of Sulu had converted to Islam, as had the court in Mindanao island and the influence of Islam slowly moved north to the island of Luzon where the Manila region was under the control of an Islamic ruler.

Spanish rule

In 1494 the Pope endeavoured to settle the commercial and political rivalries of Europe's major powers, Portugal and Spain, by determining that Spanish expeditions should sail westwards and Portuguese expeditions eastwards of an imaginary north/south line in the middle of the Atlantic ocean. Hence, Portugal established colonies in Africa, India, Malaya, the Indonesian archipelago and on the China coast, while Spain moved into the New World, establishing a base in New Spain, present day Mexico, and from there moving to conquer much of Central and South America. In the 16th and 17th centuries Mexico was a valuable source of silver and gold, carried across the Atlantic Ocean to Spain in great galleon fleets.

The Spanish explorer Ferdinand Magellan led an expedition that became the first to circumnavigate the globe in 1522. Magellan did not survive and was killed in the Philippines. A few years later another expedition arrived in the Philippines in search of the fabled spice islands. The spice islands were in what are now known as the Malukas in the Indonesian archipelago. They had long been the source of expensive spices traded in Europe. Spanish, Portuguese and later Dutch merchants dreamed of acquiring control of the spice islands in order to monopolise the supply of spices to Europe. The dreams of the Spanish expedition were shattered when they discovered that Portugal had beaten them to it in 1512. The world proved to be spherical rather than flat as believed at the time when the Pope mediated the deal between Portugal and Spain. Sailing east the Portuguese had arrived in the Indonesian archipelago a decade before the Spanish.

Other expeditions were sent to the western Pacific by the Spanish governors of New Mexico, but it was not until 1564 that the New Mexican governor decided to occupy the Philippine islands. Two motives drove the Spanish to the Philippines. First, a determination to spread the Faith. Second, the possibility of opening new trading posts and expanding trade to Asia. The first Spanish settlement was on the island of Cebu in the southern Philippines in 1565. In 1571 Spanish headquarters were moved to Manila, then a thriving entrepot dominated by Chinese merchants. Thus began more than three hundred years of Spanish influence on the Philippines. The islands were named after the Spanish Crown Prince Felipe, quickly becoming known as the Philippines.

In the 17th century Spain tried to create an Asian trading empire, based on Manila as both an entrepot and a naval base from which it could challenge the Dutch in the Moluccas. The attempt failed. Spanish economic and political power steadily declined and Spain was no match for the resurgent northern European protestant nations of Britain and the Netherlands, both of which aggressively sought Asian empires. The economic base of Spanish occupation of the Philippines in the 17th and 18th centuries was the galleon trade between the Portuguese port of Macao on the south China coast, Manila and Acapulco in New Mexico. It underpinned the Philippines until the Mexican Revolution in 1820 brought it to an end. The first Spanish governor of the Philippines, Miguel Legaspi, admired the fine Chinese silks traded at Manila by Chinese merchants and recognised a commercial opportunity for Spanish merchants to supply silk direct to the European market by exchanging silk for Mexican silver and gold. Great galleons left Acapulco for Manila laden with silver. In Manila the silver was exchanged for Chinese silk brought across from Macao. The silk was then transported to Acapulco and on to Europe, where it graced the lives of the European elite, in the process providing very profitable returns to the traders.

Manila was quickly transformed from a small but busy port town linked to regional trading networks into one of the major colonial port cities in Southeast Asia. Its rival in the 17th and 18th century was Batavia (Jakarta). In the 19th century Singapore outstripped both. Chinese merchants controlled Manila's trading lifeblood, although their numbers were only small. At the beginning of the 19th century there were probably no more than four thousand Chinese in the Philippines, mostly based in Manila. Many of the Chinese married locally and over time became a *mestizo* community. 17th and 18th century Manila was in many ways a Chinese city, or at least a city of Chinese and *mestizos*. They organised the entrepot trade and provided the internal trading and credit networks essential to that trade. There was never a large Spanish population in the Philippines and most who lived there resided in Manila. Most came via New Mexico and many were themselves creoles who married locally in the Philippines. The *mestizo* communities, one Spanish derived and the other Chinese derived, became the most powerful political and economic forces in the Philippines.

While Spanish rule in the 16th, 17th and 18th centuries had little economic impact on the peoples of the Philippines its political and religious impact was considerable. In contrast to European invaders elsewhere in Southeast Asia, the Spanish were not confronted by indigenous states supported by bureaucracies, aristocracies or religious organisations. Spanish rule defined the modern state of the Philippines and its social, religious and ideological underpinnings. Spanish power was centred in Manila on the island of Luzon in the northern part of the island chain. Despite constant efforts throughout the eighteenth and nineteenth centuries to conquer the southern islands, Spain was repeatedly rebuffed by the Islamic Sultanate of Sulu. The Sulu Archipelago and the island of Mindanao were not incorporated into the Philippines until the Americans took over the colony from Spain at the end of the nineteenth century. Even then it was only a partial incorporation. Independent Philippine governments from the 1940s to the 1990s have struggled to assert control over the Muslim south, tying up much of the Philippine armed forces in the effort to do so.

The key to Spanish control of the Philippines was the close relationship between state and church. Spain wanted to convert the peoples of the Philippines for the glory of God. Priests from Spanish orders, predominantly Jesuits, Dominicans and Columbians, were sent by the state to the countryside where they proselytised the faith and at the same time established the presence of the colonial state. Indeed, the friars were the state outside Manila, controlling large tracts of land, which they developed into plantations, and exercising considerable temporal powers alongside their spiritual powers. The people in the northern and central islands of the Philippines were gradually converted to Catholicism, albeit a Catholicism incorporating pre-catholic animistic beliefs, symbols and ritual.

From the late 18th century and through to the early 20th century social and economic structures in the Philippines were transformed. The Philippines, along with the rest of Southeast Asia, was drawn into the world trading system. The catalyst was Britain's occupation of Manila in 1762. Spain had allied itself with France in the latter's war with Britain. Britain occupied Manila in order to prevent a French threat to its China trade. Manila was sacked, galleons were captured and bullion confiscated. The British naval forces quickly departed leaving behind a considerably poorer Spanish colony. In the context of a general decline in Spain's economic power in the 18th century successive Spanish governors were forced to seek new sources of wealth and revenue.

One initiative was to create a state controlled tobacco monopoly in northern

Luzon. Local people were forced to provide labour on tobacco plantations, producing cheap tobacco for export to European markets and generating considerable profits for the treasuries of both the Philippines colony and the Spanish motherland. Another was the ending of the galleon merchants' trading monopoly. The Philippines was opened to private traders and investors. In addition to the encouragement of private traders, in 1785 the Spanish Crown established The Royal Philippine Company which became an investor in export crops in the Philippines, primarily sugar, coffee, indigo and pepper. In all of these crops the Philippines was competing on world markets with the Netherlands East Indies.

The speed of social and economic change quickened after the end of the Napoleonic War. After the colony was opened to foreign traders and investors, the Philippines could be described as an Anglo–American colony flying the Spanish flag and by the 19th century Anglo–American merchant houses dominated the burgeoning export economy. The Philippines became a major producer of cash crops for international markets with the volume of international trade increasing fifteen times between 1825 and 1875. The major exports were sugar, tobacco, coffee and abaca.

The incorporation of the Philippines into the world economy had two important consequences. First, it saw the emergence of Filipino nationalism and with it the emergence of a modern nation state. Second, it created regional economic, social and political forces that served in the long term to weaken the country. The growth of an export economy led to the creation of powerful regional elites who became the major political forces in the 20th century.

Filipino Nationalism

The Philippines nationalist movement was the earliest of its kind in Southeast Asia. Many of its leaders saw their movement as a beacon for other Southeast Asian colonies. In reality it had little impact. Nationalism took a decidedly different course in the Philippines than elsewhere in Southeast Asia. Philippine intellectual and political elites identified themselves more with Spain and later the United States than they did with anti-colonialists elsewhere in Southeast Asia.

Philippine export crops were grown predominantly on land owned by the Chinese *mestizo* community. The *haciendas* developed by powerful regional families were worked by tenants. The landowners became rich and powerful while the tenants became increasingly impoverished, trapped in a grossly unequal relationship with the landowners. Here lie the origins of the major Philippine families who continue to control the rural Philippines in the 1990s and from this economic base continue to exert enormous political power. Their wealth by and large continues to be based on large estates, even though many have diversified their investments in recent decades. The landed elite which emerged in the 19th century, unique in Southeast Asia for its social, economic and political power, educated their children in Spanish schools, seminaries and universities. Their Spanish-educated children, known as *ilustrados*, were influenced by the liberal reforms in Spain after 1868. From the 1870s they began to demand the same rights as Spaniards, including representation in the Spanish parliament.

Avowedly anti-clerical, they demanded the separation of state and church, the expulsion of the Spanish friars who dominated rural areas and the introduction of native clergy. Their demands were disregarded by both the colonial government and the Catholic Church. In the 1890s, disillusioned by Spain's refusal to treat them as equals and its dismissal of their proposals for social and economic reform, the *ilustrados* began to call themselves Filipinos.

They were led by Jose Rizal, a wealthy fifth generation Chinese *mestizo*. Hitherto the Spanish had appropriated the term Filipino for Spaniards born in the Philippines, referring to natives as *Indios*. The term *Filipino* now became a symbol of nationalism.

The *ilustrados* – the educated, wealthy *mestizo* elite – wanted to rid the Philippines of clerical domination in order to assume leadership of their society. In contrast to their moderate nationalism, in 1896 a rebellion broke out in Manila organised by a far more radical group known as the *Katipunan* and led by Andres Bonifacio, a relatively poorly educated Manila clerk. Fighting broke out in the Manila area between *Katipunan* forces and the colonial army. The Spanish responded by arresting not only *Katipunan* leaders but also many *ilustrados* as well. Rizal was arrested, charged with treason and publicly executed. Philippine nationalism now had a martyr.

At the same time as Spain was confronted by open rebellion in the Philippines it was fighting a major rebellion in its central American colony of Cuba. The drain on its limited resources was immense. United States intervention in Cuba resulted in the American–Spanish war. As a consequence the United States Pacific fleet sailed into Manila Bay, destroyed the Spanish fleet and laid seige to Manila. Philippine nationalists took advantage of a weakened Spain by declaring independence on 12 June 1898 under the ilustrado leader Apolinario Mabini. The Filipinos were the first people in Asia successfully to fight their colonial power and create a modern nation-state.

Unfortunately for the nascent Philippine Republic the United States decided that occupation of the Philippines would provide it with a base in the western Pacific from which it could promote its political and economic interests in East Asia. Early in 1899 warfare broke out between the Philippine Republic and the United States, eventually involving more than 10,000 United States troops. Most hostilities ended in 1901 when the United States effectively bought off the ilustrado elite, promising to maintain their wealth and power in return for collaboration with American colonial rule. However, the Muslim south remained under American military jurisdiction until 1913. Even then sporadic violence continued against American authorities for some years.

The agreement of 1901 consolidated the power of the landed Chinese *mestizo* elite enabling them to dominate the political and economic structures of the Philippines in the 20th century. It also created a Filipino elite that looked to the United States not only for economic and political patronage but also as its intellectual and cultural model. The *ilustrado* elite in the Philippines was a powerful landed elite with no parallel elsewhere in Southeast Asia. Its members' social and political power stemmed from an economic base independent of the colonial state.

United States colonialism

It has been argued that if Spain occupied the Philippines for 'the glory of God' then the United States occupied the Philippines for 'the democratic mission'. Certainly, Americans were uneasy about their status as an imperial nation. It ran counter to their self-perception as a people who had thrown off the colonial yoke to become the beacon for free, democratic and egalitarian values in the world. Americans' own history of anti-colonialism ensured that there were significant differences in United States rule in the Philippines from colonial rule elsewhere in Southeast Asia. From the start the United States made clear that its goal was to lead the Philippines to independence. Nationalism was a legitimate force, if possible to be moulded in its own image of course, but not to be distrusted and repressed. It followed from this that the role of the colonial state was to tutor Filipinos in the administration of a modern nation-state in order that they learn the skills necessary for independence as quickly as possible.

Given their views of themselves as being in the Philippines for the best of reasons – 'the democratic mission' – it is not surprising that United States colonial administrations stressed the development of education, health and democratic processes. Electoral systems were introduced at all levels of society and the national parliament was encouraged to invigilate officials and influence colonial policies. By 1934 the United States Congress mandated Philippine independence within twelve years. As a first step, in 1935 a Philippines Commonwealth was established, autonomous in domestic affairs with Manuel Quezon as its first President. Political developments in the Philippines were unique in Southeast Asia, though in the long run the effect was to increase the wealth and power of the landed elite.

The United States government expended money on the Philippines rather than extracted money from it – another unique occurrence in colonial Southeast Asia. Much of this money was spent on developing education and health systems far superior to anywhere else in the region. At home the United States was committed to mass education at all levels, in contrast to Britain, France and Holland which restricted access to high schools and believed that a University education was only for a small elite.

Education policies in the Philippines reflected American domestic educational philosophies, in the same way as education policies in British, French and Dutch colonies reflected their domestic policies. The contrast between the Philippines and Indonesia on the eve of World War II is illustrative of these differences.

In the Philippines in 1938–39 there were 7,500 students at the University of the Philippines in Manila. In the same year in Indonesia there were a mere 128 students at Colleges of Law, Medicine and Engineering. In 1941 the literacy rate in the Philippines was five times that in Indonesia.

Nationalist movements in most of colonial Southeast Asia flourished from the 1910s, demanding independence, by and large rejecting colonial cultural mores and vigorously debating the need for radical social and economic reform. They were generally led at the 'national' level by the western-educated sons of either the traditional aristocracy or the bureaucratic elite and at the local level by upwardly mobile clerks, schoolteachers and government officials. There was a wide spectrum of parties, ranging from conservative ones, which wanted independence and little social or economic change, to the communist parties which wanted revolution. The Philippines was once again an exception. Its nationalist movement was dominated by the Nationalist Party under the leadership of Manuel Quezon.

Leaders were from the landed elite, even more wealthy and powerful under American rule than they had been under Spain. While publicly demanding immediate independence, in fact their personal economic interests were well served by continued United States rule.

Enjoying self-government after 1935, and under a relatively benign colonialism, the Filipino nationalist elite remained pro-American. In many ways they were bi-cultural. The shape of Filipino nationalism – in ideology, myths and symbols – was very different from elsewhere in Southeast Asia. With no need to foster a strong 'national' consciousness and few 'national' symbols, regionalism and regional loyalties based on regional landed elites remained strong. This had significant consequences after 1945. Filipino nationalists were barely conscious of the events going on elsewhere in Southeast Asia. It left a legacy of separateness from the rest of Southeast Asia which had only partially changed by the 1990s.

Japanese Occupation

When General MacArthur was forced to flee the Philippines in 1942 he uttered the famous words 'I shall return'. When in 1944 he did return at the head of American troops charged with driving the Japanese back to Japan he was greeted as a hero. Fighting in the Philippines during the Pacific War was more intense than elsewhere in Southeast Asia. It took six months of bloody warfare for the Japanese to oust the Americans in 1941–42 and another ten months for the

Americans to expel the Japanese in 1944–45. There was a great cost in Filipino lives. Japanese slogans such as 'Asia for the Asians', 'Japan the light of Asia' and 'The Co-Prosperity Sphere' made much less sense to Filipinos than to other Southeast Asians. The nature of American colonialism, the bi-culturalism of the Filipino elite, the experience of self-government and the realisation that they were due to get independence in 1946 anyway, placed Filipino nationalists in a different relationship with the Americans than nationalists elsewhere in Southeast Asia with their colonial rulers. Though opinion was divided about the appropriate response to occupation, resistance to the Japanese in the Philippines was strong. The collaborationist government established by the Japanese lacked legitimacy in the eyes of many Filipinos.

Comparisons with other Southeast Asian countries are striking. Often the invading Japanese were seen as liberators elsewhere. The iron grip of colonial rule was broken. Certainly, the mood changed to resentment and then hatred of Japanese brutality but Japanese occupation opened the way for nationalists to seize power in August/September 1945 and to organise resistance to the re-invading Europeans. Filipino nationalists, by contrast, welcomed the returning American forces as liberators, restoring the country on the path to independence promised by 1946.

However, there were important long-term effects from the Japanese occupation of the Philippines. Its incorporation into Japan's Southeast Asia empire broke the isolation of the Philippines from the rest of the region that had begun with the arrival of the Spanish and continued through United States rule. Filipinos became more aware than ever before of their place in Asia. The war also sharpened social, economic and political tensions in the Philippines. Throughout Japanese occupied Asia people suffered badly. Filipinos were no exception. Corruption increased, the gap between the rich and the poor widened and social structures broke down. In 1946 the Communist Party of the Philippines took advantage of the deteriorating conditions in the countryside to arouse support for rebellion. The war also spawned an armed society. Filipinos put up strong resistance to the invading Japanese and the fighting between United States/Filipino and Japanese forces in 1944–45 was extensive. The violence of the war years led to a greater preparedness to use force to achieve political ends in the post-independence Philippines.

Independence and the Democratic Years

Historians of the Philippines have stressed the importance of the family to an understanding of the political structures and the political culture of the Philippines. They see independence in 1946 as changing very little. A small number of wealthy families, generally based on extensive regionally-based land holdings, has controlled Philippines politics since the first elections in 1907.

In the late 1960s a prominent Philippines businessman summed up the failure of the Philippines political system with the statement 'we have no institutional loyalty, only personal loyalty.' The political process in the 20th century Philippines – both pre- and post-independence – has been based on extensive patron-client relations, linking at the base of the society exploited peasants and powerful landlords. Party politics has been free of ideology – with the exception of the Huks and the Communist Party of the Philippines. Party loyalty has been fickle, based on a complicated and extensive reward system linking party notables to politicians and local leaders.

Between the achievement of independence in 1946 and the Marcos coup in 1972 the Philippines was a constitutional democracy with all the trappings of an American style political system. In practice, it was a system of intra-elite struggle, based on powerful patron-client relations at the apex of which were the landed families. The most serious opposition came from the Huk movement, based on support from impoverished tenant farmers and landless labourers in central Luzon. The Huks were in open rebellion against the Philippines state between 1946 and 1953. They were crushed by a combination of coordinated military activity and rural reforms introduced by President Magsaysay. However, rural discontent and unrest has remained a serious problem in the Philippines down to the present day. Local military and police forces are used by the local elites to contain rural resistance, and where they fail extensive private armies owned by the landlords are brought into play.

In the 1950s and 1960s the underlying rural problems were masked by the apparent success of the industrialisation policies of the Philippines government. The state promoted import substitution manufacturing by imposing high tariffs and import controls and by managing the exchange rate. A new industrialist class emerged. Some were from the wealthy landed elite, diversifying their capital away from its rural origins. Others emerged from professionals and traders, who created joint ventures with foreign, predominantly American, companies or with wealthy local Chinese.

By the 1960s the Philippines was the most successful manufacturing country in Southeast Asia and appeared to be the most prosperous. Urbanisation occurred apace. From the manufacturing companies built up behind tariff walls and state subsidies emerged a number of conglomerates with interests in agrobusinesses, real estate and banks as well as manufacturing. Some became multinationals.

The Marcos Era

Ferdinand Marcos was elected President in 1965 and re-elected in 1969. Neither he nor his wife Imelda came from the powerful landed oligarchy that controlled the Philippines. He was dependent on powerful and wealthy patrons for financing his electoral machine. Marcos was openly unimpressed with the democratic system, arguing that it should be replaced by what he called 'constitutional authoritarianism', a system he saw as more in keeping with Filipino political culture.

In 1972 Marcos proclaimed Martial Law. Many explanations have been advanced for this decisive break with Philippine political history. First, Marcos was constitutionally barred from standing for a third term as President. Determined to hold on to power he was prepared to destroy the Constitution. Second, the halcyon days of the 1950s and 1960s had turned sour. The Philippine economy was stagnant, per capita income was falling, foreign indebtedness had grown to serious levels and there was growing middle class discontent about political corruption and the inability of the political system to solve the country's social and economic problems. Third, the military leadership was willing to become more directly involved in running the country. Military leaders welcomed the suspension of democratic processes and the increased power that flowed to them as a consequence.

Many Filipinos also initially welcomed Marcos' move. The New Society promoted by Marcos was attractive to many of the urban middle class and intellectuals. It promised 'law and order' in a hitherto insecure society; it promised to provide the infrastructure and stability needed to attract the foreign investment essential to revive the economy; it promised land reform and an end to the corruption that had bedevilled the Philippines since independence. Martial Law was also welcomed by outsiders, including foreign investors, the United States government and other Southeast Asian governments, most of which were themselves in various degrees military-dominated regimes.

Initially, the Marcos dictatorship did stimulate increased foreign investment and a return to economic growth. However, by the early 1980s new economic and political weaknesses had become obvious. Under the guise of creating a New Society, Marcos systematically undercut the political power of the landed elite at both national and local levels. Businesses of his political opponents were confiscated, licenses withdrawn and state enterprises became part of the Marcos personal fiefdom. He was able to do all of this because he had the support of the military leadership.

The beneficiaries, apart from the Marcos' themselves and favoured military leaders, were a small group of friends and relatives who were provided with lucrative monopolies, government contracts and cheap finance. 'Crony capitalism' was taken to spectacular heights by the late 1970s. Through all of this Marcos and his family acquired enormous personal wealth, with the removal of the boundary between state finances and personal income. Corruption and nepotism were practiced on an unprecedented scale.

While the landed oligarchy lost their political power Marcos ensured that their economic interests were protected. Land reform and an end to rural impoverishment remained mere rhetoric.

Marcos centralised state power but did not create an institutionally strong state. The power of the state depended on personal loyalties, primarily from army commanders to Marcos. By the 1980s the Philippines was a society in danger of falling apart. The Moro Nationalist Liberation Front (MNLF) in the south had 50–60,000 guerrillas fighting for an independent Muslim state. More than half of the Philippines army was engaged in fighting it. The remainder was engaged against the New People's Army (NPA), the communist-controlled front organisation which by the mid-1980s had about 15,000 guerrillas and was able to launch commando style raids in towns and cities, including Manila. Opposition to Marcos became more public and more strident.

In August 1983, Benigno Aquino, Marcos' most prominent and popular political opponent, returned to the Philippines from his exile in the United States. He failed to set foot on Philippine soil. As he descended the steps from his aircraft at Manila airport one of the accompanying soldiers assassinated him. The military leadership denied involvement, as did Marcos. The death of Aquino began a process of open resistance to Marcos, a resistance led by the Manila middle class.

Under pressure from the United States and still supremely confident of his ability to fix elections, Marcos called a snap Presidential election for early 1986. Despite the vote rigging he lost. In a few chaotic months in Manila, Cory Aquino, the widow of Benigno Aquino, claimed victory and prepared for an inauguration organised by her supporters. Marcos continued to claim victory, despite all the evidence to the contrary, and moved towards his own inauguration. The imminent danger of serious bloodshed, if not outright civil war, was averted when a number of significant army leaders deserted Marcos and moved over to support Aquino. Marcos fled the Philippines. Cory Aquino became President. 'People power' had won.

The restoration of democracy

With the end of Martial Law, the exile of Marcos and the inauguration of Cory Aquino, Philippines politics returned to its pre–1972 Constitutional form. The continuities of Philippines political life remained. The landed gentry retained their wealth and restored their political power. Many of those who lost out under Marcos have restored their fortunes. The great families still dominate the Philippines. Despite Aquino's promise of land reform the interests of the landed elite have prevailed. Land reform has been negligible. Political loyalties remain personal rather than institutional. Electoral success continues to depend on wealthy people funding corruption, nepotism and bribery. The state remains relatively weak, as compared to many of the neighbouring ASEAN countries.

There have been, however, major achievements since 1986. Not least were the peaceful and constitutionally correct elections in 1992 which brought Fidel

Ramos to power as President. On the economic front, the first four or five years of the Aquino government saw an impressive economic turn-around from the negative growth of the last years of Marcos to a positive growth which peaked at 6.7 per cent in 1988. The growth fell away after 1990, in part because of the deteriorating world economy and the economic dislocation caused by the Gulf War, but in part also because of the failure of basic infrastructure such as power to keep up with demand. By the mid 1990s the Philippines had been restored to economic growth levels approaching those achieved elsewhere in ASEAN. But it has a long way to go before it is seen by foreign investors as competitive with other ASEAN countries.

The threats from the NPA and the Moro Nationalist Liberation Front have receded considerably, if not disappeared altogether. With the end of Marcos rule much of the discontent that fuelled support for the NPA dissipated. Clever political accommodation by the Aquino government, together with more effective army action, has for the moment ended any NPA threat. The Moro Nationalist Liberation Front has been handled equally skillfully, though it remains to be seen whether the present agreements have staying power. Much depends on whether Muslims in the south can be persuaded to feel part of the Philippines which, in turn, depends on central concessions to regional, cultural and religious differences as much as continued economic growth.

TIMELINES

1990: Goh Chok Tong becomes the countries second Prime Minister

1965: Leaves Malaysia and becomes independent Republic with Lee Kuan Yew first Prime Minister

1963: Joins with Malaya to form Malaysia

1959: Elections result in People's Action Party gaining a majority that was to begin their period of dominance of government in subsequent elections

1955: Limited self government granted

1948: Malay Communist Party launches insurrection in Singapore and Malaysia resulting in a State of Emergency being declared

1942-45: Japanese occupation

1890s: Established as a major trans-shipment port and commercial centre

1867: Straits Settlements become a Crown Colony

1842: Britain's annexation of Hong Kong accelerates Chinese migration

1826: Straits Settlements formed with Penang and Melaka

1819: Stamford Raffles arrives and establishes English East India Company

ASEAN FOCUS GROUP

Singapore

Singapore is an immigrant society. When acquired by Britain in 1819 it was populated by only a few hundred Malays living simple lives in fishing villages. In the 1990s it is a thriving city-state, with a population of about 2.7 million, and a per capita income the highest by far in Asia outside of Japan.

Geography is central to Singapore's history. Located at the foot of the Malay peninsula, separated from the mainland by a narrow stretch of shallow water, it is the pivotal island in the Straits of Melaka. Singapore's history has revolved around turning its strategic location to its commercial benefit while remaining on good terms with its larger neighbours.

Singapore is a Chinese city-state. There is a significant Indian minority, and a much smaller Malay community, but political, commercial and cultural power is in the hands of the ethnic Chinese. A major theme in Singapore's history since the end of the Second World War has been the continuous efforts to create a Singapore identity. What does it mean to be a Singaporean? How can the predominantly Chinese cultural heritage be transformed into a distinctly Singaporean culture? How best can a small, predominantly ethnically Chinese island relate to its overwhelmingly more populous Malay-Muslim neighbours in Malaysia and Indonesia?

Colonialism

Stamford Raffles hoisted the British flag on the island of Singapore on 29 January 1819. It was the second island in the region occupied by the English East India Company (EIC). Penang had been acquired in 1786. The EIC had a monopoly on the English trade between India and China, had acquired considerable territory in India and was eager to ensure control of the Straits of Melaka, the crucial passage of water through which most of its trading ships to China sailed. Penang gave it the ability to control the northern entrance of the Straits: Singapore gave it the ability to control the southern exit.

For nearly two hundred years the Netherlands East Indies Company, the VOC, had been the EIC's arch rival in the region. When Napoleon annexed the Netherlands in 1810, Britain occupied the major Dutch possessions in the Indonesian archipelago in order to prevent them falling into the hands of the French. Melaka, Bencoolen on the west coast of Sumatra and the island of Java were taken over by Britain. Stamford Raffles was appointed head of a civil government to run Java and Sumatra. The colony was added to the EIC Indian empire, reporting directly to Calcutta.

When the Napoleonic war ended in 1815 Britain wanted to bolster the Low Countries (the Netherlands and Belgium) as a bulwark against a revived France.

Dutch pressure, then, for the return of its colonies in the Indonesian archipelago fell on responsive ears. In 1818 Java was returned to Netherlands rule. Raffles was extremely disappointed that wider European strategic considerations had forced him to return Java to the Dutch. He was an expansionist at heart, believing that Britain should acquire territory throughout the Indonesian archipelago and the Malay peninsula, create European settler societies and reap the benefits of what he saw as enormous commercial opportunities. On being forced to leave Java he turned to a small island off the southern tip of the Malay peninsula, known locally first as Temasek (Sea Town) and later as Singapura (Lion City), persuading the Sultan of Johor to cede it to Britain. Sparsely occupied by Malay fishing communities and by Malays better known for their activities as pirates in the local waters, there were no more than one thousand people on the island in 1819. In 1826 the EIC amalgamated Singapore, Penang and Melaka into the Straits Settlements, administered from Singapore. The Straits Settlements remained in EIC control until 1867 when they became a Crown Colony under the control of a Governor appointed by the Colonial Office.

The British commercial community were strong supporters of the acquisition of Singapore, seeing it as a boost to trade in Southeast Asia. In 1824 the Anglo–Dutch Treaty settled territorial disputes between the two countries, with the Netherlands recognising Britain's possession of Melaka and Singapore and Britain handing Bencoolen back to the Netherlands. By the 1830s Singapore had become the major trading port in Southeast Asia. It was challenged by Manila and Batavia (now Jakarta) but had three crucial advantages over the other colonial port cities and over the major indigenous ports.

First, its geographic location: most ships trading between China, India and Europe had to pass Singapore. Second, its status as a free port: the Dutch in Batavia and the Spanish in Manila levied a range of tariffs and charges on imports as did local rulers in the smaller ports. Third, its linkages into the British commercial and industrial empire: by the nineteenth century Britain was the dominant colonial power.

Singapore was an integral part of Britain's empire in Asia, although the centre of the empire was India. Its prosperity stemmed from its geographic advantages and from its place in the colonial network. British traders were attracted in ever increasing numbers and major trading houses, shipping lines and service companies quickly emerged. Equally importantly, Chinese traders long resident in Southeast Asia were attracted to Singapore because of its free port status, the certainty of the British legal system and the strategic position of Singapore.

Many came from Melaka and the Riau archipelago in the 1820s, relocating their trade to Singapore and thereby immediately linking Singapore into indigenous regional trading networks. Malay, Indian and Arab traders were also drawn to Singapore from other ports in the vicinity. Singapore quickly gained a dominant share of the inter-island regional trade as well as becoming the major victualling stop en route to China. Chinese traders had worked in the region and had settled in Chinese quarters in all of the major port cities well before the arrival of the Europeans. Their numbers increased greatly from the seventeenth century as first the Dutch and the Spanish and later the British and the French colonised the region. But it was not only colonised Southeast Asia that attracted Chinese traders, entrepreneurs and labourers.

Thailand's kings encouraged the migration of Chinese in the 19th century, as did the Sultans of the Malay States. Indeed the tin mining industry which developed in the Malay States from the 1830s was created by Chinese who worked under concessions granted to them by Malay rulers. The tin miners imported their needs through Singapore and used Singapore to export tin ore to the world. Tin mining in the Malay States, and in southern Thailand, was the source of wealth for a number of Chinese families who later went on to become major traders and financiers in the region.

The Chinese were the labour force on which British Singapore was built and Singapore was the conduit for the hundreds of thousands recruited to colonial Malaya and the Netherlands East Indies. Most Chinese came to Singapore as impoverished indentured labourers. The forced opening of the Treaty Ports in southern China and Britain's annexation of Hong Kong in 1842 accelerated the migration of Chinese from southern China to Southeast Asia, Australia and the Pacific and the United States.

The migration flow was organised and exploitative, with male Chinese signed on as indentured labourers. In the nineteenth century the Chinese population of Singapore was predominantly male. Most came to Singapore hoping to make a fortune, send money back to families in their home villages in China and one day themselves return home, to marry, buy land and live as prosperous farmers. Some succeeded. Most lived and died in Singapore as coolie labourers, reliant on prostitution for female company and dependent on Secret Societies, opium dens and gambling parlours.

Singapore's economic history is interwoven with the economic history of the Malay States. The Singapore merchant community started to advocate British acquisition of the western Malay States from the 1840s. Chinese and Europeans in Singapore were significant investors in the tin mining industry in the western Malay States and were increasingly frustrated at what they saw as the political instability of the Malay States and consequent lost commercial opportunities. Britain finally began to acquire control of the western Malay States in 1874 when the ambitions of the Singapore merchant and financial community were bolstered by imperial fears of French and German intentions in Southeast Asia. Singapore was a major beneficiary of the addition of Malaya to the British empire.

By the late 19th century Singapore was an important financial and commercial centre. It was a major trans-shipment port, where the products of Southeast Asia were collected, packaged and re-exported and from where the products of industrial Britain and Europe were distributed. On the eve of the Second World War over two-thirds of Malaya's imports and exports went through the port of Singapore: it had also become a major financial and commercial base for British companies in Southeast Asia.

Investment in tin mines in the Malay States was matched from the 1890s by investment in rubber plantations and on the transport infrastructure needed to get rubber to the ports for export. Investment finance came through Singapore, tin and rubber were exported through Singapore and Singapore was the warehousing and distribution centre for the imported goods needed by the growing European population.

The largest commercial firms were British owned and managed. But there also emerged a growing number of Chinese owned enterprises. Some were trading companies, others were financiers and yet others were small scale food processors and distributors. By 1942, when the Japanese invaded Singapore, there were a number of strong family companies in Singapore owned by second or third generation Chinese.

While most Chinese immigrants who began life as rickshaw coolies or wharf labourers ended their lives much as they started, a few realised the immigrant's dream of making good. These Chinese enterprises were family companies linked into the commercial and financial network of the Chinese diaspora in Hong Kong and other parts of Southeast Asia.

There was little manufacturing in Singapore before 1960. There was some food processing, primary processing of tin and rubber originating in Malaya and simple manufacturing, such as shoes and clothing. However, as late as 1960 between 70 and 75 per cent of Singapore's workforce was engaged in the service sector. In the early 1930s a government appointed commission investigated the possibility of Singapore developing an industrial base but concluded that it was only feasible with high levels of protection and if the Singapore and Malayan economies were united. It concluded that the losses to Singapore from abandoning free trade status would outweigh the gains from a protectionist industrial policy.

Singapore was an immigrant colony, however by the 1931 census, 36 per cent of its residents had been born in the Straits Settlements. Immigration restrictions in the 1930s, as a consequence of the Depression, led to 60 per cent of Singapore residents being Straits born in 1947. Nevertheless, with the exception of the elite, the mother tongue and language of day-to-day communication for the Chinese remained southern Chinese dialects.

By the early 20th century there were nationalist movements demanding independence in most Southeast Asian colonies, from Burma through to the Philippines. Singapore was an exception. There was no sense of being Singaporean: people identified themselves as Chinese or Nanyang Chinese (Overseas Chinese). There was, therefore, no clearly articulated movement seeking the creation of an independent nation-state. Although the Malayan Communist Party (MCP) operated in Singapore in the 1920s and 1930s, as well as in British Malaya, and was involved in organising among Chinese and Indian workers, it made no attempt to develop a specifically Singapore identity or nationalism.

Political activity in Singapore in the 1920s and 1930s was focussed on the struggle between the Chinese Communist Party (CCP) and the Kuomintang (KMT) for control of China. Both the CCP and the KMT gained ideological and financial support from the overseas Chinese. Singapore was a particular focus of propaganda and recruitment. Politically aware Chinese in Singapore were far more concerned about the great events convulsing China in the 1920s, 1930s and 1940s than events in Singapore. Whatever their ideology, they were united in opposition to Japan's invasion of China in the 1930s.

Chinese communities throughout Southeast Asia were caught up in the events of their homeland and the battle for the hearts, minds and pockets was waged throughout the region. One important difference in Singapore was that because the dominant culture was Chinese, and to all intents and purposes there was no indigenous society, Chinese nationalism could focus on the ideological struggle in China unencumbered by an indigenous nationalist movement. Chinese communities elsewhere in Southeast Asia were equally concerned about events in China but were forced by the existence of strong nationalist movements to ask fundamental questions about their individual and communal identities and their place in an independent nation.

Colonial Singapore was a European city. Its ruling elite, its commercial core and its official ethos was British. But beyond the European homes, clubs and offices the island was culturally predominantly Chinese. There was, however, a significant Indian minority, varying from 6 to 12 per cent of the population in the colonial era. This minority was large enough to create its own communities where the visitor would clearly be aware of moving out of the dominant Chinese society into a 'little India'.

The Indian community was far from united. The major divisions were between Hindus and Muslims and between southerners and northerners, but these were cross-cut by further divisions of caste and region. Some of the early Indian settlers came from Penang, where there was a thriving Indian commercial community. Others migrated from India or were recruited as indentured labourers. Many thousands were forcibly transported from India as convict labourers. Until 1873 Singapore was partially used by British India as a penal colony. Indian convicts built the early government buildings, roads, bridges and drainage systems. In the 19th century free Indians were primarily in public employment, such as clerks, teachers and policemen, or were merchants and moneylenders.

Like the Chinese majority, the political attention of Indian residents in

Singapore was focussed on the motherland where Indian nationalists were locked in struggle with the British Raj. The political divisions which opened up in India in the 1920s and 1930s were reflected in the Indian community in Singapore. Muslim and Hindu, Sikh and Bengali, to name but a few, each had their own, often conflicting, view of Indian politics. While there was considerably more crossing of caste and ethnic divides in the Singapore Indian community than in India itself, nevertheless these divisions remained important barriers. Indian communities in Singapore were linked by region, language, caste and family to the much larger Indian community in British Malaya, adding yet one more strand to the interconnection between Singapore and Malaya.

On the eve of the Pacific War, Singapore was a multi-racial, multi-lingual and multi-religious society governed by a British elite. Social control was maintained not merely by the police and court systems but also by the pro-British Chinese business and clan heads and by the wealthy leaders of the Indian community. It was a key part of the British empire: arguably the most important commercial possession east of India and from the 1920s a major naval base guarding British interests in Southeast Asia and providing a defence shield for Australia and New Zealand.

The Japanese Occupation

Singapore fell to the Japanese Imperial Army on 15 February 1942. The loss of this strategically important island in Southeast Asia quickly led to the capitulation of the Netherlands East Indies. Thousands of Europeans, civilians as well as soldiers, were trapped in Singapore. Many were dispatched to build the infamous Thailand–Burma railway. The death rate was high. Over 45,000 soldiers in the Indian and Malay regiments were urged by the Japanese to transfer their loyalties. Most refused. Many paid for their refusal with their lives. About 20,000 Indian soldiers joined the Indian National Army in the belief that it would be prepared by the Japanese to drive the British out of India and establish Indian independence.

The Chinese, Indian and Malay communities in Singapore suffered greatly at the hands of the Japanese. None more so than the Chinese. The Japanese military distrusted all Chinese, and in particular sought to root out all who were Kuomintang supporters. Arbitrary arrests, torture and executions were commonplace. Special taxes were imposed on Chinese incomes and assets. For the residents of Singapore the Japanese occupation was a time of struggle to survive. British rule was benign by comparison.

The Japanese occupation of Southeast Asia greatly reduced European prestige. Indeed, while historians differ as to the long-term impact of the occupation on individual societies, there is general agreement that it ushered in the beginning of the end of European colonialism in the region. Japanese policies and actions clearly impacted greatly on individuals in Singapore. Apart from the Chinese, Indians and Malays who died in prisons, in labour camps or as a result of indiscriminate Japanese brutality, almost all who lived there suffered severe day-to-day hardships during the three and a half years of Japanese occupation. The deeper, long-term impact is harder to assess. A legacy of distrust of Japan in Singapore and throughout Southeast Asia may well be the most significant consequence.

Towards Independence

Britain re-occupied Singapore in August/September 1945. Until mid 1946 it was controlled by the British Military Administration and then handed back to the Colonial Office. Post-war British policy towards Singapore differed from that towards Malaya. It envisaged Malaya moving towards independence but was determined that political reform in Singapore should be carefully controlled with a restricted goal of limited self-government. There were three main reasons for this policy difference. First, continued direct control of Singapore was seen as vital to British commercial interests in Southeast Asia. Second, Singapore was a strategic naval base in Southeast Asia. Third, Singapore's ethnic Chinese majority raised fears for British interests, not just in Singapore, but also in Malaya. The outbreak of the Cold War in 1947 and Mao's defeat of the Chiang Kai-Shek government in China in 1949 strengthened Britain's view of Singapore as potentially a communist fifth column in Southeast Asia. It was believed that an independent Singapore would quickly come under communist control and that Singapore would then be used as a springboard to subvert western interests in Malaya, Indonesia and elsewhere in Southeast Asia.

The Malayan Communist Party's (MCP) success among Singapore workers in the immediate post-war years confirmed the British view of Singapore as inevitably a hotbed of Chinese communism unless strong colonial rule was maintained. The pro-British Chinese and Indian elites were equally alarmed: communism threatened their interests as much as it did the interests of the British. The MCP launched its insurrection in Singapore and Malaya in 1948, resulting in a declaration of a state of emergency which lasted until 1960. The strength of communist controlled labour unions in the late 1940s and early 1950s and the MCP's insurrection were viewed in the context of growing pride among overseas Chinese in the achievements of the communist government in China. The victorious communists and the nationalists vanquished to Taiwan competed vigorously in the 1950s for moral support from the overseas Chinese. Singapore was again a vital hub in the Southeast Asia campaign.

Limited self-government was introduced into Singapore in 1955. In 1959 the People's Action Party (PAP) gained a majority of seats in the Legislative Assembly, beginning a dominance of Singapore politics continuing to the present day. Led by Lee Kuan Yew, a young Cambridge educated lawyer, the PAP was a party of a new English-educated elite emerging in Singapore in the 1950s. Strongly influenced by European social democratic ideas, the PAP developed a blueprint for Singapore's development based on a strong state and state intervention in the economy to create a new industrialised Singapore. Lee and his fellow PAP leaders knew that their strongest opponents were the communists, operating through various legal and illegal structures and in the early 1960s most prominently through the Barisan Socialist party. The organisational structure of the PAP mirrored that of communist parties. Its democratic centralism placed effective control in the hands of a self-selecting elite.

By the early 1960s, Britain was searching for a way to end its direct rule of Singapore while still safeguarding its strategic and commercial interests which were seen as inextricably connected with preventing Singapore from 'going communist'. The pressure for Singapore independence was strong. In addition, Britain was faced with the problem of the Borneo states of Sabah and Sarawak. In an era of decolonisation Britain had to find a solution to its colonial problems in Singapore and Borneo.

The creation of Malaysia seemed to solve all problems. Singapore, Sabah and Sarawak would be amalgamated with Malaya to form the new state of Malaysia. The Chinese majority in Singapore would be balanced by Malay and other indigenous majorities in Malaya and the Borneo states. It was a neat political solution. It was also seen by both the British and the Singapore elite as a consummation of the strong economic interdependence that had developed between Malaya and Singapore over more than a hundred years.

Singapore would retain control over a number of crucial areas, including education and communications, in return for a lower proportion of seats in the new federal parliament of Malaysia than it was entitled by weight of population. Malay sensibilities about dominance by ethnic Chinese appeared to be assuaged and at the same time the PAP ensured a status for Singapore far greater than that of a mere State Government.

Malaysia was formed on 16 September 1963. Singapore separated from Malaysia in September 1965, becoming the independent Republic of Singapore. Formally, the exit of Singapore from Malaysia was a mutual decision between the Malaysian Federal Government and the Singapore State Government. In reality Singapore was forced to leave. The two years of marriage were unhappy ones. Malays increasingly feared that Singapore wanted to dominate Malaysia, and that the PAP was trying to join forces with the major ethnic Chinese opposition party in peninsular Malaya in order to gain a majority of the seats in the federal parliament. They feared changes to the constitution, which entrenched major privileges for the Malays. It was a highly emotional two years, with inter-ethnic typecasting abounding and with Malays fearing that 'their' country was about to be taken over by 'foreigners'.

Lee Kuan Yew was personally shattered by the exit of Singapore from Malaysia. The accepted wisdom in Singapore was that its economy was so closely linked to that of peninsular Malaya that economic prosperity depended on these links continuing. Singapore feared that its economy was too small and too vulnerable to anti-Chinese feelings among neighbouring Indonesians and Malays to stand alone. Thirty years later Singapore is a major economic success story. Since independence in 1965 its economy has grown at an average of nine per cent per annum. In 1988 per capita income was almost ten times that of 1965. This economic growth is the cornerstone of the generally high standing of the PAP government among Singaporeans, despite western complaints about its style and frequent disregard for 'western style' civil liberties.

Even before independence the Singapore government led by Lee Kuan Yew determined that the economy had to undergo massive structural change very quickly if Singapore was to prosper. In thirty years Singapore has moved from an essentially entrepot economy to a predominantly industrial economy. The next thirty years will see Singapore move into a post-industrial phase with most of its wealth generated by service industries, ranging from providing regional financial and high technology services to other Southeast Asian nations to manufacturing high technology products for a world market.

The quite remarkable and sustained economic growth in post-independence Singapore is partially explained by Singapore's strategic location at the crossroads of the ASEAN region. ASEAN countries have also experienced sustained high growth rates to Singapore's advantage. As labour intensive industries have moved from Singapore to other ASEAN countries they have been replaced by a regional reliance on Singapore for more technologically sophisticated products and services. There are other important factors behind Singapore's success. First, the PAP has brought strong, stable and corruption free government to Singapore. Above all, Singapore has been a model of planned development in every sphere. Second, through policies such as the creation of a Central Provident Fund, with Singaporean employers and employees compelled jointly to contribute up to forty per cent of salaries to a pension fund, it has created a very high rate of national savings. Third, it has adopted social policies which have ensured that all Singaporeans have benefited from the economic growth. For example, when the PAP came to power in 1959 most Singaporeans lived in squalid housing. By the mid 1990s Singapore has the highest home ownership rate in the world, thanks to the activities of the Housing Trust and the ability of people to fund mortgages by borrowing from their contributions to the Central Provident Fund. Fourth, it has developed an excellent comprehensive education system which has produced the skilled workers needed to sustain high rates of economic growth.

Government in Singapore is far more intrusive that that experienced in western societies. Some commentators allege the PAP has made it difficult for an opposition party to challenge its power. From time to time the Internal Security

Act (brought in by the British) has been used to arrest and imprison those who are considered a threat to the State. Many western observers (and a growing number of Singaporeans) consider the government to be paternalistic and, at times, authoritarian but, despite this, there is absolutely no doubt the government does have popular legitimacy because of its delivery of clean government and its impressive social and economic achievements over thirty years.

Over the past thirty years the Singaporean government has been concerned to develop a Singaporean identity. In the first instance, this meant weaning Singaporeans away from too close an attachment to communist China. Language policy was a key part of this search for a Singapore identity. In the 1960s the stress was on the need for people to learn Malay and English, with government sponsored campaigns to learn a new Malay word each day.

As Singapore's prosperity grew, as the economy became more internationalised and less dependent on Malaysia, and as China became less of a threat and more of a source of pride, policy shifted towards the promotion of Mandarin instead of regional dialects. More recently the emphasis has moved back to ensuring the survival of regional dialects alongside Mandarin and English.

If Singapore's elite was uncertain about its identity in the 1960s and 1970s – were they simply Chinese overseas or a genuine part of the region? – by the 1980s they were far more confident about Singapore's future in the ASEAN region and by the 1990s supremely confident of their ability to continue to prosper in a increasingly global economy and within the strongly developing Southeast Asia region. Some commentators have talked of a re-signification, not just of the Singaporeans, but of ethnic Chinese communities throughout Southeast Asia as they network with each other and continue to have a dominant role in national and regional economies.

In the 1990s Singapore is by far the most prosperous nation in Southeast Asia (aside from the aberration of the tiny State of Brunei). It is a society full of contradictions. In many ways it is a modern Confucian state – mostly paternalistic, sometimes authoritarian and with a strong ideology of the people's duties towards the state. It is ruled by a close knit meritocratic elite focussed on the PAP. The State claims the right to be involved in all aspects of its people's lives: asserting the right to influence family size and the nature of personal relationships as well as to determine the structure of the economy.

The State directly owns or controls large sections of the economy and through a government owned investment company has shares in other Singaporean companies as well as overseas. Yet it is also the champion of free enterprise, welcoming foreign multinationals and nurturing its own multinational corporations. It has an enviable record in providing low cost housing, high quality education and extensive health care for all Singaporeans. Yet its social security net is almost non existent, insisting that individuals must work hard and stand on their own feet. It is a state which encourages aggressive economic activity, and rewards individual ability and achievement. Yet it is a puritan state, with a state controlled local media, strong censorship of foreign media and a very public concern about moral pollution of the young from western cultural influences.

Singapore's prosperity gives it a higher per capita income than many western countries and by the beginning of the twenty first century it will be among the three or four most prosperous societies in the world. Its geographic location may be less important in the global economy with the advent of the computer revolution, yet in regional terms is still as important as ever. Singapore's enthusiastic participation in a growth triangle with Malaysia and Indonesia reflects its view of itself as the economic engine of the region.

The Singapore government still worries about national identity, with repeated campaigns focussing on one or other aspect of the ideal Singaporean. It is also in the 1990s in the process of rediscovering its past, in part for tourist reasons but also as part of the continued search for a national identity.

TIMELINES

1973-92: Between Autocracy and Democracy

1948-73: The 'Strong Man' Era

1932-48: Rise of Military Governments

1910-32: Eclipse of the Role of the Monarcy

1868-10: Modernisation under King Chulalongkorn

1857: King Mongkut signs Bowring Treaty

1782: Chakri Dynasty commences

1767: New capital at Thonburi

1351-1767: Ayudhya Kingdom

1279-1298: Sukhotai Kingdom

Mid-late 13th century: Small kingdoms across northeast Myanmar, central and northern Thailand and Lao

7th-13th century: Tai migration south from western and northern China

Thailand

Thailand stands at the heart of mainland Southeast Asia, yet its modern history differs strikingly from the turbulent history of the rest of the region. Culturally Thailand's population (approaching 60 million in the early 1990s) is relatively homogeneous; no major regional, ethnic, linguistic or religious rifts have threatened national coherence. Thailand does harbour minorities, but it is well on the way to assimilating its most significant minority, the Chinese. Uniquely in Southeast Asia, Thailand avoided the disruptions of Western colonial rule – and, therefore, the upheavals of decolonisation. World War II produced no serious conflict on Thai soil. After the war, and unlike in neighbouring Indochina, communism never attracted wide support in Thailand. While revolution was tearing Vietnam, Lao and Cambodia apart, and military-imposed 'Burmese socialism' was stifling Burma, Thailand embarked on capitalist development which by the 1990s had made it one of Southeast Asia's strongest economies and brought it close to the status of a NIC (newly industrialised country).

Historically the Thais have nevertheless had to face serious problems. In the 18th century Thai society had to rebuild itself after the trauma of almost total destruction by Burmese armies of the four-centuries-old Thai kingdom of Ayudhya. In the 19th and early 20th centuries Western pressures forced major, but necessarily delicate, adjustments to traditional Thai government, the economy and social organisation. In World War II Thailand had to adjust to Japanese military pressures, and the country suffered acute economic disruption. Afterwards Thailand became a frontline state in the Cold War, its fortunes tied closely to United States' interests.

Until 1932 Thailand was an absolute monarchy. Subsequently it experienced a succession of unrepresentative military-dominated governments. A violent collision between the military and pro-democracy demonstrators on the streets of Bangkok in 1992 may have ushered in an era of representative democracy, but this is not yet assured. Resolution of conflict about the form of Thai government is needed, for the country is again facing problems. The country's economic successes have been impressive, but they have forced change on Thai society at a headlong pace. Pressing problems include inadequate infrastructure, an overburdened metropolis in Bangkok, serious pollution and ecological degradation, deplorable conditions for many workers, and widening gaps between urban and rural, and rich and poor, Thais.

Thais sum up their social coherence in the nationalist prescript 'Nation, Religion (Buddhism) and King'. They are proud of their history, out of which these nationalist symbols have emerged. This history is worth studying for clues about the ability of the Thais to handle their present difficulties.

Early history

In the 13th century several small kingdoms emerged across the regions known today as northeast Burma, central and northern Thailand, and Lao. These were probably the first attempts at state-building by Tai communities. The Tais were the principal ancestors not only of today's Thais but also of the Lao peoples, the Shans of Burma, a range of upland communities in mainland Southeast Asia such as the Black, Red and White Tais of Lao and northern Vietnam, and the Lü of Yunnan, China.

It used to be thought that, before the 13th century, Tais had dominated a kingdom called Nanchao in Yunnan, but had been dispersed southwards by a Mongol attack in 1253. Scholars no longer hold this theory. Instead the evidence suggests long, slow Tai migration over many centuries, beginning in western China, or even further north, and spreading southwards from the 7th century.

The Tais were wet rice farmers clustered in *muang* – one or more villages under a chieftain. Over time some *muang* developed inter-relationships cemented by trading networks, intermarriage, security needs and talented military leaders. But the 13th century leap from linked *muang* to kingdoms was propelled by Tai adaptations of beliefs, ideas and techniques derived from the states and empires they were encountering in their southward movement. The Tais probably adopted Theravada Buddhism from Mon states in what is now central Thailand and from the Burmese kingdom of Pagan. This religion accommodated itself to Tai folk traditions and animist beliefs but it was also an institutionalised religion with a universalist world view and a transmitter of Mon, Burmese and Sinhalese civilisation.

The principal blueprint for Tai state-builders was, however, Angkor, the great Cambodian kingdom which at its height from the 11th to 13th centuries dominated an empire stretching from the Mekong delta to the northern Malay peninsula and as far north as the Vientiane plain. From Angkor came ideas adapted originally from Indian Brahmanical thought, particularly concepts of society as a divinely ordained hierarchy and of *devaraj* – the ruler as an immensely potent incarnation of a Hindu deity and/or Buddhist boddhisattva. Angkor also provided lessons in administering large, scattered populations and in a range of arts and technologies.

Tai attacks upon Angkor's imperial outposts, and eventually upon Angkor itself in the 14th and 15th centuries, would lead to a direct transfer to them of human and material resources. Meanwhile in the 13th century the most celebrated of early Tai states was the kingdom of Sukhothai. Modern Thais regard Sukhothai as the birthplace of the Thai nation, particularly under Ramkhamhaeng, king c.1279 – 1298, whose rule is celebrated by the Sukhothai stone – an inscribed obelisk reputedly discovered in 1833 by the Thai prince Mongkut, then a monk and scholar and later Thailand's first modernising monarch. The inscription portrays Sukhothai as an idyllic place, governed by a just, fatherly and devoutly Buddhist monarch. Possibly it is Ramkhamhaeng's self-justifying counterblast to the arrogance and avariciousness of imperial Angkor. In recent years the stone's authenticity has been questioned, some sceptics arguing that Mongkut himself devised the inscription to give his people an appealing early history. Scholarly consensus continues to view the inscription as genuine, however.

The kingdom of Ayudhya, 1351–1767

After Ramkhamhaeng's death Sukhothai dwindled in significance. In 1351 the establishment further south of the kingdom of Ayudhya – or Siam as it came to be known – would provide a more lasting basis for Thai statehood. As Siam's capital, Ayudhya would survive for over four centuries, until 1757. It was founded by U Thong, who is thought to have been a Chinese merchant who acquired wealth and prestige from his trading connections with the Chinese imperial court.

He was related by marriage to a prominent Thai family, and he emphasised his devotion to the Thai form of Buddhism. He may be an early example of a repeated theme in Thai history – the readiness of Thai society to absorb talented Chinese and other foreigners. The people over whom U Thong claimed kingship in 1351 were perhaps predominantly 'Tai', but 'Thai-ness' was also being constructed out of Mon, Khmer, Chinese and other people.

Ayudhya prospered, partly because of its strategic position. It stood only 70 kilometres up the broad Chaophraya River from the sea, enabling it to become one of Southeast Asia's great trading ports. Simultaneously it commanded the vast, fertile Chaophraya plain, providing rice for a growing population and for export. The city's power was also based on its rulers' keen attention to government and social control. From the beginning they insisted that male subjects pay many months of service each year to the state, as soldiers or labourers; a concept which became known as *corvée* labour which was used in a number of European countries, especially France.

King Trailok, who reigned from 1448–88, elaborated to an extraordinary degree the place and duties of subjects in a rigidly hierarchical society. Codifying the structure of government and the civil law, Trailok developed the system of *sakdina*, which carefully scaled the positions of everyone in the kingdom. The pyramid social structure which resulted was intended to enforce social discipline and enable the easy mobilisation of manpower. The structure was legitimated by a parallel hierarchical organisation of the *sangha* (Buddhist monks) under royal patronage and oversight.

Elements of the *sakdina* conception of society persist in Thai thinking, and are indeed embedded in the Thai language. However, automatic social obedience was probably never absolute in Ayudhya. The elaborate delineation of social standing bred a self-conscious concern for dignity in even the most humble individual, resulting in at least passive resistance to unjust superiors. Other question-marks against the cohesion of Ayudhyan society concern the regional dispersal of administrative and military power, and the difficulties surrounding monarchical succession. Ayudhyan history would be marked by rivalries between powerful families, each with bases in the provinces, and by clashes over a vacant throne.

Even so, Ayudhya's social structures proved remarkably strong and enduring. Manpower conscription enabled military-minded kings to defeat Angkor decisively, wage war on other regional rivals, and to claim an empire sometimes encompassing much of modern Lao, the Tai kingdom of Lan Na, based on Chieng Mai (Thailand's second largest city), and the states of the Malay peninsula. In the 15th and 16th centuries Cambodia remained a significant antagonist, but Ayudhya's main challenges would come from the Burmese. Only the strong institutions of Ayudhyan society would enable it, indeed, to survive the blows dealt it by the Burmese.

In 1568 the Burmese King Bayinnaung laid seige to Ayudhya, having extended his military power over the north as far as Lao. The city fell in 1569 and was destroyed. Yet over the next decades Narasuan, heir to the throne, managed to reconstitute the kingdom and as king in 1593 decisively repulsed a renewed Burmese attack. In succeeding years he clawed back much of Ayudhya's tributary empire, and by the early 17th century Ayudhya was again a major power.

European reports provide a striking picture of 17th century Ayudhya as a famed and wealthy trade centre. By then Portuguese, Spanish, Dutch, French and English traders jostled there with Chinese, Japanese, Persian, Indian, Malay and other Asian traders. Ayudhya's openness to trade – and to the information and ideas that traders brought – may have been one of the sources of its strength. In 1688, however, the nobility split over the degree of foreign influence at court, particularly that of an extraordinary Greek adventurer Constantine Phaulkon, who had become a powerful minister; and of the French, including French Jesuit missionaries. Upon the death of King Narai a relatively minor official, Phetracha, organised a coup, excluded the French and had Phaulkon executed. Phetracha assumed the throne himself. Agitation over these events and the legitimacy of Phetracha's subsequent dynasty would dog Ayudhya for the next 80 years.

It was possibly ruling class divisiveness which accounted for Ayudhya's poor response to its greatest challenge – another, and massive, Burmese beseigement in 1766. In April 1767 the city fell, to an enemy set on destroying Thai state power forever. Ayudhya's ruling class was decimated. Tens of thousands of people and all portable wealth were carried off. The city was burned. Vast tracts of territory were left as scorched earth by the Burmese forces.

The rise of the Bangkok empire

This time of crisis saw two remarkable Thai military leaders emerge, Taksin and his leading general Chaophraya Chakri. Taksin had a Thai mother and Chinese father. He had been raised at court and in 1767 was a provincial governor. In the leadership crisis following the destruction of the old regime Taksin rallied an army, imposed his authority on a distracted people, declared himself king and founded a new capital at Thonburi. During the 1770s he and his armies rebuilt an empire which included Chieng Mai in the north. In 1778 armies under Chaophraya Chakri subdued Luang Prabang (the old capital of Lao) and captured Vientiane (the modern capital of Lao). From the latter city they brought back the Emerald Buddha, subsequently Thailand's most sacred, and it is believed most potent, Buddha-image.

In his later years Taksin undermined respect for his imposing achievements with viciously tyrannical behaviour. He may have succumbed to religious dementia, for he alienated the *sangha*. In 1782 a tax revolt evolved into a coup, and Taksin was deposed and executed. The coup leaders offered Chaophraya Chakri the throne, thus inaugurating the dynasty of Thai monarchs which continues to the present.

Rama I (reigned 1782–1809) had been born of a Thai father – a relatively minor Ayudhyan official though of aristocratic lineage – and a Chinese mother. He would prove to have not only military skills but great administrative and intellectual abilities. Militarily his reign would see the triumphant, and final, repulsion of the Burmese in 1785 and 1786, and the consolidation of a Thai empire larger than any Ayudhya had controlled. Effectively it covered all of mainland Southeast Asia excluding Burmese and Vietnamese territory, and also included the northern Malay states. Local dignitaries ruled at the empire's perimeters – in Cambodia, Lao and the Malay states – but they did so at the Thai king's behest.

At home Rama I supervised the construction of his new capital Bangkok, founded in 1782, which soon became a major cosmopolitan port. From Bangkok the king rebuilt administrative structures reminiscent of Ayudhya's but arguably even stronger. Labour control now involved mass registrations and the tattooing of subjects to indicate place of residence and administrative superior. Rama I gathered about him talented officials, jurists, scholars and artists. With them he revitalised Thai culture. Their achievements included the reconstruction and reform of the *sangha* hierarchy, the production of a new, definitive text of the Buddhist scriptures, the complete revision of the kingdom's laws, and the translation of numerous literary and historical works including the Indian epic *Ramayana* (in translation, Ramakian).

The king and his followers self-consciously renovated, rather than merely restored, old institutions. The Bangkok court thus moved into the 19th century demonstrating an intellectual and cultural acuity that would be of incalculable value in the years ahead.

Bangkok and the West

Unlike island Southeast Asia, where the Dutch had been extending their empire since the 17th century, mainland Southeast Asia did not encounter intense Western pressures until the 19th century. Even Rama I's successors Rama II (reigned 1809 – 24) and Rama III (reigned 1824 – 51) were largely able to ignore or turn aside the problems presented by the increasing Western presence in the region. Rama III did reach vague agreement with a British emissary in 1825 (at a time when the British were conquering southeast Burma) about reducing and standardising the taxes on trade. He was unwilling, however, to grapple with the major legal and administrative changes which Western businessmen, perplexed by Thai customs and Asian ways in general, were calling for.

In key respects, therefore, Bangkok remained 'traditional' in the first half of the 19th century. This was most obvious in its vigorous prosecution of its authority over its empire. By military intervention in the Malay peninsula it risked tensions with the British, ensconced from the 1820s in the Straits Settlements and lower Burma. In the 1830s and 1840s Bangkok saw as its chief foreign threat not any Western power but Vietnam. Between 1841 and 1845 it fought an exhausting struggle with the Vietnamese over control of Cambodia, a struggle ending effectively in a stand-off.

Virtually at the centre of Bangkok society, however, a group of royal and noble young men were studying the West keenly, led by the example of Prince Mongkut, brother of Rama III. Then a monk, Mongkut was devoting much of his energies to the ongoing reform of Thai Buddhism. He founded the *Thammayutika* sect, whose goal was intellectually rigorous religious scholarship, clearing away additions to original Buddhist teachings. Mongkut and his circle were also studying Western languages, Western science and mathematics, and such matters as Western military organisation and technology. When Mongkut succeeded to the throne he was therefore in a position to reorientate Bangkok positively towards the West.

King Mongkut (Rama IV, 1851–68) signed the Bowring treaty with Britain in 1855. Under this treaty import and export duties were sharply reduced and fixed, ruling class trading and commodity monopolies were abolished, and British subjects were granted extra-territorial legal rights. In subsequent years Mongkut signed similar treaties with many other Western powers. The signing away of legal power over foreign subjects in the kingdom was a bitter blow – these rights would not be fully recovered until the 1930s. More crucially, the other provisions of the treaties deprived the throne and many powerful subjects of much income. The shortfall would be reversed in time by the expansion of trade and by heavy taxes on opium, alcohol and gambling, but it is testimony to Mongkut's domestic diplomatic skills, and to the cohesion of his court, that the major fiscal rearrangements passed without revolt.

Mongkut avoided other fundamental reforms. The 'modernisation' of the kingdom would really only begin with his son Chulalongkorn (Rama V, 1868–1910). Even then it would be cautiously undertaken and limited in scope. Chulalongkorn learned caution early in his reign. In 1873, at the age of 21, he announced some financial and legal reform measures which alarmed conservatives and provoked an attempted coup in 1874. The young king survived, but had to rein in his reforming enthusiasm. A strategy for the gradual abolition of slavery, also announced in 1873, continued however. Slavery disappeared over the next decades, although not always the bonds of patronage and obligation in Thai society which slavery had formalised. Later Chulalongkorn was also able to phase out *corvée*, replacing it with a capitation tax.

Chulalongkorn's position grew stronger as the older generation passed on and he matured into a shrewd politician, nurturing a corps of bright, Western-educated royal relatives. With them he set about major reform of government in the mid 1880s. Functionally specialised ministries and departments began to appear. Cabinet government was introduced between 1888 and 1892. Subsequently the king's half-brother Prince Damrong undertook the delicate task of reforming provincial administration, placating the great regional families while centralising bureaucratic control in Bangkok.

The modern look to government came none too soon, for Western imperial rivalries in Southeast Asia were reaching their peak. Chulalongkorn's skilled foreign minister, Prince Devawongse, could now put the case that the kingdom had no need of Western intervention – unlike its neighbours it was stable, bent on modernisation and able to accommodate international business. Even so, Western empires stripped the former Thai empire. Already Mongkut had been obliged by the French in 1867 to abandon claims to Cambodia, except its western provinces. Now in 1893 (when French warships menaced Bangkok) and in 1902 and 1904 Chulalongkorn had to transfer to the French sovereignty over the areas which would constitute modern Lao, and in 1907 relinquish the western Cambodian provinces. In 1909 he gave control to the British of four northern Malay states formerly under his suzerainty (this left, nevertheless, a Malay-Muslim minority within his kingdom). Meanwhile, an 1896 treaty between France and Britain had marked a crucial turning-point in the disposition of Thai territory. This treaty, designed primarily to head off Anglo–French confrontation in Southeast Asia, guaranteed the independence of most of the territory which today forms Thailand. Chulalongkorn's core kingdom had been secured.

He proceeded with modernisation until his death in 1910, laying the foundations of a modern military, improving communications – particularly with an extensive railway system – and continuing law reform. Western-style education became common for royal and upper class children, and an elementary Western-style syllabus was introduced in the temple schools. Chulalongkorn resisted full-tilt modernisation, however. He rejected any thought of introducing democracy. Economically he presided over the development of a quasi-colonial state. Ordinary Thais became commodity producers for the world market, rice accounting for over 70 per cent of exports in the early 20th century. Other items included tin, teak and rubber. There was no significant industrialisation. Western and Chinese interests dominated the country's financial and commercial life. Chinese numbers swelled to about 10 per cent of the population. The size and power of the Chinese community began, indeed, to disturb many Thais.

The eclipse of the monarchy, 1910–1932

During the reigns of Chulalongkorn's successors Vajiravudh (Rama VI, 1910–25) and Pradjahipok (Rama VII, 1925–35) disgruntlement with Thailand's equivocal modernisation and economic subjection would grow amongst the expanding, though still small, Western-educated elite. Vajiravudh's *dilettante* approach to kingship also provoked criticism. His inner circle at court consisted of male favourites. His extravagance contributed to government deficits and a balance of payments crisis in the 1920s. On the other hand, his contributions to the emergence of Thai nationalism probably strengthened his reign. He introduced the trinity of 'Nation, Religion (Buddhism) and King' as the focus of popular loyalty, and promoted organisations and public spectacles designed to inculcate nationalist pride. In the 1920s he also sponsored successful diplomatic efforts to end the extra-territoriality provisions of Mongkut's treaties and recover national control of tariffs.

Prajadhipok (Chulalongkorn's 76th child – Vajiravudh died heirless) took an earnest approach to his duties, but was hamstrung by the financial problems bequeathed to him and even more by the Great Depression. In the early 1930s national income slumped, and cuts to government expenditures heightened discontent. For him the promotion of nationalist thinking proved to be a double-edged sword. The concept of 'Nation' alongside that of 'King' soon encouraged modern-minded Thais to distinguish between the two. On 24 June 1932 plotters in the military and bureaucracy staged a coup – carried out without bloodshed – and, in the name of the nation, obliged Prajadhipok to surrender the monarchy's absolute powers and accept constitutional status. In 1935 Prajadhipok abdicated in favour of his nephew Ananda (Rama VIII, 1935–46) who was then at school overseas and would remain abroad until 1945.

The rise of military government, 1932–1948

The promoters of the 1932 revolution consisted of both civilians and military men. Their professed goal was the staged introduction of parliamentary democracy, and they set up a National Assembly of appointed and elected members. By the late 1930s, however, the parliament appeared doomed to virtual irrelevancy. For 60 years after 1932, in fact, the military would dominate Thai government.

For several reasons military dominance would not prove stifling nor produce wholly negative effects. Firstly, Thai military leaders faced no serious problems of national integration; history had bequeathed to them a country of relatively minor cultural, religious, ideological or ethnic tensions, and they could usually enforce their will with a relatively light hand. Secondly, they would generally be willing to accommodate other elites in the power process, and those elites – business, bureaucracy and civilian politicians – would generally acquiesce in military preeminence. Thirdly, ossification of the power structure would be avoided, crudely but not ineffectively, by rivalries within the military and changes of government by intra-military coup. Finally, successive military-dominated governments would pursue modernisation, economic growth and the expansion of education and other services. For several decades this would seem to justify military rule – though it would eventually undermine it. Economic development and a better educated society would finally produce broad-based pressures for more representative government.

In the 1930s Thailand was still overwhelmingly a country of peasant farmers. The military was its best-organised, most cohesive modern institution. The military's crucial place in the 1932 revolution was underscored in October 1933, when pro-royalist protesters marched on Bangkok. They were repulsed by troops commanded by a Lt Colonel Phibun Songkhram. The following year Phibun became Defence Minister. He would then hold various posts until he became Prime Minister in 1938, heading a cabinet of predominantly military men.

Phibun and his supporters, unimpressed by the floundering Western democracies of the period, were attracted to other political models – fascist Italy, Germany and above all Japan, the one Asian country which seemed to offer Thailand a pattern for modernisation. Phibun rapidly adopted some features of dictatorship, arresting opponents, promoting himself as Thailand's great leader and exciting nationalist emotions. A series of 'cultural mandates' attempted instant economic and social change. Domestically his most dramatic move was legislation aimed at the Chinese in Thailand. State corporations took over commodities such as rice, tobacco and petroleum, and Chinese businesses found themselves subject to a range of new taxes and controls. Chinese economic know-how was in fact too valuable for anti-Chinese measures to be pushed far, but Phibun's policies would have lasting effects. They stimulated Chinese assimilation into Thai society, through Sino-Thai business partnerships, intermarriage, and Chinese acceptance of Thai language, education and culture. They also set in train heavy state involvement in the economy, which would blur the lines between business and those who held political and bureaucratic power.

Pursuing his nationalist goals, Phibun changed his country's name from Siam to Thailand in 1939 (the name Siam would be briefly resumed between 1945 and 1949). Phibun pointed out that 'Siam' was originally a term for the area used by Chinese and other foreigners, but the change also had irredentist implications – should 'the land of the Thais' include 'Tai' people who lived beyond its borders, many as a result of Western pruning of the old Bangkok empire? Phibun answered this question in November 1940, when Thai forces invaded Lao and western Cambodia. The Japanese, who now held base and transit rights in French Indochina, stepped in to mediate, awarding Cambodia's western provinces and portions of Lao to Thailand.

This victory was popular in Thailand. Phibun's subsequent relations with the Japanese would become more controversial. In December 1941 the Japanese moved troops into Thailand, demanding transit rights for their attacks on British Burma and Malaya. Thai troops resisted, but the Phibun government called for a ceasefire within hours. Subsequently it entered a military alliance with Japan and in January 1942 declared war on the United States and Britain. Division about these events within Thai ruling circles was indicated most obviously by the refusal of the Thai Minister in Washington, the aristocratic Seni Pramoj, to advise the United States government of the declaration of war. A Free Thai movement began to grow amongst overseas Thais and eventually underground within Thailand itself.

At first, however, Phibun's actions were widely supported, and Thailand was rewarded by Japan with the Shan states of Burma in 1942 and the four northern Malay states in 1943. Disillusionment began to set in as the tide of war turned against Japan, and Thailand experienced acute economic disruption because of the war. In July 1944 Phibun quietly resigned the prime ministership, leaving the National Assembly with the problem of preparing Thailand for an Allied victory.

The politicians were restrained by the Japanese presence until August 1945, but then all agreements with Japan were repudiated (including those which had transferred territory to Thailand). The goal of democratic government was reasserted. A range of factors would, however, frustrate the achievement of that goal. The British and French were at first bitterly hostile to Thailand. The economic difficulties of the war years persisted. Political infighting prevented effective or even stable government.

In the midst of the turmoil King Ananda, who had returned to Thailand in December 1945, died of a gunshot one morning in June 1946. His death has remained shrouded in mystery. The young king enjoyed collecting guns and most likely the shot was self-inflicted by accident, but the political scene was inflamed by murder theories. The Prime Minister Pridi Phanomyong, famed as the chief civilian promoter of the 1932 revolution but viewed by conservatives as a radical leftist, resigned amidst mounting hysteria against 'communists'. Government continued to flounder until the military stepped in, staging a coup in November

1947. Initially they retained a civilian Prime Minister, but forced him to resign in April 1948. He was replaced by Phibun.

The 'strong man' era, 1948–1973

The resumption of military dominance over government initiated a succession of authoritarian leaders unchallenged by forces outside the military until 1973. Their power was enhanced by United States patronage and aid. Washington wanted strong anti-communist leaders who would both repress domestic communism (never more than a fringe phenomenon in Thailand in fact) and join in American-led strategies for the containment of Asian communism. From the 1950s United States aid to Thailand was substantial. It enabled much social and economic development, notably in communications, infrastructure and social welfare projects, but it also bolstered military and police power.

Even so the goal of stable government was not necessarily secured. American aid created new opportunities for corruption in Thai government and administration, and stimulated competition for the prizes of power between rival political networks anchored in the military but reaching into business and the bureaucracy. American appeals for some evidence of democracy in Thailand produced, in the short term, only cynical political manipulation, rigged elections and rubber-stamp parliaments from time to time.

After 1948 Phibun resumed many of his former repressive policies. He mounted another anti-Chinese campaign, and also attempted to impose cultural uniformity forcefully on the Malay-Muslims of the far south. The latter resisted the arrival of Thai officials, the introduction of Thai-language education and the substitution of Thai law for customary law. A separatist movement grew which, despite conciliation by later Thai governments, would persist to the present.

Despite the tough image which Phibun once more projected, his power was not in fact secure. He faced several attempted coups from within the military between 1948 and 1951. All were defeated, but at the price of the emergence of two further 'strong men' – army commander, subsequently Field Marshal, Sarit Thanarat (whose later spectacular wealth would be grounded in his control of the government lottery) and police chief Phao Siyanon (who would make his fortune from opium trafficking). In 1955 Phibun eased the controls on political activity and promised elections. Possibly he was under American pressure, possibly he hoped to outmanoeuvre his rivals by winning popular endorsement. However his party was accused of massive fraud during the 1957 election. Sarit won popularity by resigning, supposedly in disgust, from Phibun's government. In September 1957 Sarit staged a coup, driving Phibun and Phao into exile.

In October 1958 Sarit declared martial law, silencing the experiments in open politics since 1955. Sarit justified his authoritarianism in two ways – he argued for a return to Thai traditions of social order, and he accelerated economic development and social modernisation. Under the former banner the monarchy was given renewed prominence.

King Bhumibol Adulyadej (Rama IX, 1946–present) attended public ceremonies, toured the provinces and patronised development projects, becoming a personally revered figure. Under the banner of development, Sarit introduced to government a new generation of economically liberal technocrats, encouraged private and foreign investment, launched major rural development programs and rapidly expanded educational facilities.

When Sarit died in December 1963 power transferred peacefully to his close associates Generals Thanom Kittikachorn (who became Prime Minister) and Praphas Charusathian (Deputy Prime Minister). Thanom and Praphas basically maintained Sarit's style of government and economic policies, which produced GNP growth rates of over 8 per cent per year during the 1960s. At the same time the military's place in the Thai political landscape seemed to loom larger than ever. United States aid increased sharply because of the Indochina conflicts. From 1964 Thailand provided bases for the United States airforce and committed its own troops to action in Vietnam and Laos. United States aid was also forthcoming to combat a communist insurgency which had taken root amongst alienated tribal groups in the country's north and northeast.

The era of unquestioned 'strong man' rule was drawing to a close, however. Economic development, wider education and better communications were rapidly increasing the numbers of the politically aware. In 1968 Thanom proclaimed a new constitution, and in 1969 an election established a new parliament. The political public was shocked when he reversed direction in 1971, dissolving the parliament and banning political parties once more. By the early 70s several other issues were raising concern. The leaders' presumed successor, Narong Kittikachorn (Thanom's son and Praphas' son-in-law), was not regarded highly inside or outside the military. Thailand's close involvement with the United States obviously required rethinking as the United States moved to disengage from Vietnam and the region. The OPEC 'oil shock' and rising prices sent tremors through the economy.

It was the educated young who precipitated the downfall of the Thanom-Praphas regime. In October 1973 student protests against political repression (inspired to some extent by the Western student radicalism of the era) escalated into massive confrontation with the police on the streets of Bangkok. Popular sympathy for the students increased when police killed or wounded several students. In the first subtle indication of royal political opinion in many years, the King permitted student first-aid stations on royal ground. The demonstrators triumphed when the army withheld its support from Thanom, Praphas and Narong, who fled into exile.

Between autocracy and democracy, 1973–1992

The 'Students' Revolution' unleashed an extraordinary burst of political activism. Political parties mushroomed, hitherto banned ideas circulated freely, trade unionism flourished, and numerous organisations of all shades of opinion set out to politicise the people. Even the Buddhist *sangha*, long a compliant supporter of government, revealed radical dissent within its ranks.

An interim civilian government arranged for a fully elected parliament to be created by elections in January 1975. The result was an unstable coalition government which collapsed within twelve months. Another ineffective coalition emerged from elections in April 1976. Meanwhile the problems of a destabilised economy were not being addressed, nor the apparent threats to Thailand from the communist victories in Cambodia, Vietnam and Lao in 1975.

Conservative opinion, outraged by the political disorder from the beginning, increasingly became popular opinion. In October 1976 the military resumed power unopposed, permitting right-wing organisations to torture and kill student radicals gathered at Thammasat University in Bangkok. Many leftist and moderate leaders fled the city, some to join the communist insurgents in the northeast.

For the moment it appeared that Thailand faced more authoritarian government than ever before. The policies of the first post-coup Prime Minister, a civilian but a rigid right-winger, deepened rather than healed the divisions in the country. Even civil war seemed possible, if the newly expanded insurgent forces could attract popular sympathy.

Within the military, however, opinions varied after the 'Students' Revolution' about the future of Thai politics and the military's relationship to government. At one pole of a spectrum of opinions stood those keen to retain the autocratic discipline of the 'strong man' years. At the other stood those who saw the development of democracy as desirable, even inevitable; clearly Thai society was now unwilling to be politically passive. In the middle of the spectrum, key military figures concluded that 'managed democracy' was possible. This has remained an option attractive to military politicians ever since. Management may include a range of strategies: the maintenance of a constitution allowing for an appointed Prime Minister, appointments to other senior posts and a part-appointed parliament; the nurture of political parties sympathetic to military interests; the promotion of the military to the public as an efficient national institution more likely to deliver government in the common good than self-interested (civilian) politicians. The strategy of managed democracy also seemed to require, however, that the military should retain the right to the ultimate weapon of political management, the coup.

In October 1977 General Kriangsak Chomanand assumed the Prime Ministership, promising a new constitution and elections in 1979. Kriangsak also offered amnesty to repentant insurgents. This helped to speed the collapse of an insurgency movement increasingly disillusioned in the late 1970s by the falling out between Cambodia, Vietnam and China, and by the revelations of the horrors of Khmer Rouge rule in Cambodia. (Ironically it would be the Thai military, rather than the insurgents, who would develop a liaison with the Khmer Rouge, after Vietnam's occupation of Cambodia in 1979.)

Not long after the 1979 elections Kriangsak was succeeded by General Prem Tinsulanonda, whose form of managed democracy would attract the label 'Premocracy'. Prem was an appointed Prime Minister (under the 1978 constitution) but he took care to base his authority on parliamentary support, persuading MPs from a range of parties to back him. Generally, Prem maintained a reputation for being 'clean' and making appointments to senior posts on the basis of merit. Military elements twice tried to overthrow him, in 1981 and 1985, but on both occasions he survived with the explicit support of the King and of loyal military forces.

Prem retired in 1988 and elections brought to power a civilian Prime Minister, Chatichai Choonhavan, heading a coalition identified with civilian political and business interests. The Chatichai government was buoyed by economic boom conditions and initially by popular enthusiasm, and the military took a 'wait and see' attitude. Military leaders grew alarmed, however, when Chatichai manoeuvred to diminish their influence behind the scenes. Pro-military media publicised, with relish, examples of his government's inefficiency and undoubtedly grave corruption. In February 1991 a quiescent public observed a well-planned coup which overthrew Chatichai, parliament and the constitution.

The principal figure behind the coup was army commander General Suchinda Kraprayoon; other leading figures included the navy and air force chiefs and the deputy commander of the army. Their alliance dated back to their education at Chulachomklao Military Academy, where they had graduated as members of 'Class 5', a generation of cadets which had come to dominate many key positions of power. The coup group – calling themselves the National Peacekeeping Council (NPC) – set out to explore new methods of managed democracy, promising another constitution and elections, and establishing an interim government headed by Anand Panyarachun, a respected businessman and former diplomat. The NPC's stance may have been prodded by more than domestic considerations. Many countries expressed dismay at the 1991 coup. International business indicated some alarm at the capriciousness of the Thai political scene.

As interim Prime Minister, Anand performed effectively, but controversy grew over the new constitution announced in December 1991, which favoured the military by allowing for an appointed Prime Minister and an appointed upper house (the Senate) with power over legislation. The NPC leadership proved able, however, to command the lower house too. Elections in March 1992 gave a narrow majority to a coalition of parties supporting, or willing to align themselves with, military-dominated government. Only the question of a Prime Minister seemed to remain.

The military's initial choice for Prime Minister, a civilian lower house MP, had to withdraw when the United States government publicised his links to the drug trade. General Suchinda stepped into the vacuum – to the outrage of Thailand's frustrated democrats. Mass demonstrations began in Bangkok, led by the Buddhist ascetic Chamlong Srimuang, an ex-military officer and former Bangkok Governor. Chamlong had a reputation for incorruptibility. With his political party Palang Dharma and its supporters he now campaigned for clean, democratic government. In Bangkok and major provincial centres they enjoyed wide support.

Disastrously, Suchinda ordered troops to use force against the demonstrators. Between May 17 and 20, 1992 at least fifty protesters were killed (several hundred according to rumour at the time) in scenes of mayhem and military brutality that shocked television viewers around the world. On May 20 the King intervened. A truce was negotiated which led to Suchinda's resignation as Prime Minister, after he had declared an amnesty for 'all parties' involved in killing and injuring demonstrators. Anand returned as interim Prime Minister, minor modifications were made to the constitution, and fresh elections were scheduled for September 1992.

Anand took the opportunity of the military's discomfiture to remove Suchinda's fellow coup leaders from their positions of power. The September elections gave a narrow majority to anti-military parties (Democrat, New Aspiration, Palang Dharma and Solidarity). Democrat leader Chuan Leekpai, a lawyer, assumed the Prime Ministership. He subsequently strengthened his control of the lower house by wooing another party, Social Action, into his coalition. His government has remained encumbered, however, by an unelected Senate, which on matters of constitutional reform can unite with opposition MPs in the lower house to block further progress towards a fully democratic political system.

Thailand in the 1990s

The wave of domestic and international revulsion against the violence of May 1992 diminished the likelihood of further direct military intervention in Thai government. However, the wish of democratic reformers to detach the military from politics and other non-military spheres of public life will not be easily achieved. Long years of military dominance have taught the present officer corps to expect influence, careers and rewards beyond the strictly military realm. Constitutional reform to reduce military management of parliament remains to be achieved.

Military political influence remains particularly strong in rural Thailand, where the armed forces present an image of practical concern for development and for the needs of the poor. Meanwhile civilian politicians still need to convince many Thais that they put clean, stable and effective government ahead of their personal interests. Corruption is a spectre which hangs over civilian as well as military politics.

It must also be a matter of concern that the monarchy has had to involve itself in politics in recent years. The present King has acted judiciously and maintained broad national respect, but royal intervention in politics raises risks, for the monarchy and for social stability if an intervention were to be misjudged. Thailand's political system cannot be seen as stable or mature while resort to royal arbitration remains an occasional necessity.

Today some Thais also fear for another traditional source of social stability – Buddhism. In pre-modern Thai society Buddhism, as well as providing religious inspiration and solace, was probably the chief form of 'social cement'. Buddhist temples were centres not only of worship but of education and social activity. Royal and aristocratic patronage of Buddhism ensured that the traditional social order enjoyed religious legitimation. In 1902 King Chulalongkorn formalised the administration of the sangha (Buddhist monks), in effect making the *sangha* an arm of the state. Post-1932 governments perpetuated this strategy; both Phibun and Sarit reorganised *sangha* administration, at least in part for political purposes.

In the short term the strategy enhanced social order. In the longer term it has produced scepticism amongst many Thais towards established Buddhism and its conservative teachings. This has led in some cases to indifference, in others to the growth of movements and sects challenging mainstream Buddhism. Modern education and rising affluence have of course contributed to the diversification of attitudes towards religion.

Instabilities in Thai society can be exaggerated however. Despite the intermittent political crises at the top, Thai society has remained serenely stable when compared with neighbouring countries. This stability has enabled economic and social development on a breathtaking scale. The political discord of recent decades may have reflected strains and tensions arising from rapid social change, but it has never endangered Thailand's development more than fleetingly.

For over three decades Thailand has achieved average annual growth rates of around 7 to 8 per cent, reaching over 10 per cent in the late 1980s. The country has been a favoured destination of foreign investment, led at present by Japan and Hong Kong, with Taiwan, the United States and Singapore also posting significant shares. Meanwhile Thai investment also now flows to other countries of the region. Virtually a rice-growing mono-economy before World War II, Thailand's economy is now broad-based, producing a range of agricultural products, many of them processed in Thailand, and manufactures. Mining and oil/LNG constitute a growing sector. The growth of manufacturing has been the most spectacular aspect of the development. Negligible till the 1950s, manufacturing accounted for over 26 per cent of GDP in the early 1990s and dominated Thailand's exports. By then agriculture had shrunk relatively, to around 12 per cent of GDP. With such growth Thailand has become a key regional financial centre. It is at present the only member of ASEAN in mainland Southeast Asia. Thai business expects to play a significant role in the development of southern China, Vietnam, Lao, Cambodia and Burma.

Within Thailand other major changes have been taking place. The population stood at 38 million in 1970 and 57 million in 1991 (the annual growth rate is now down to 1.2 per cent however). Improved medical and other services have significantly reduced the death rate and the incidence of malnutrition, tuberculosis and tropical diseases. In education, enrolment rates have grown at all levels, far outstripping population growth at secondary level (up fourfold between 1970 and 1990) and tertiary level (up eightfold). A trend to urbanisation, reflecting economic shifts, has meant that about 40 per cent of Thais now live in Bangkok or provincial towns. In the capital and other urban centres the emergence of a substantial consumer-oriented middle class is strikingly evident.

The old Thailand, where small royal, aristocratic or military elites could dominate a quiescent population of subsistence farmers, has gone.

Thai government must now grapple with an increasingly mobile, affluent and educated society. Other problems loom as large. The agenda of issues confronting any Thai government today seems, indeed, disconcertingly long and urgent. On a macroeconomic level Thailand must move on from industrial development based on cheap labour and foreign-owned technology. Meanwhile the present boom has produced extreme disparities of wealth, both vertically and horizontally. The affluent share the cities with workers on minimal wages, frequently labouring in atrocious conditions. When income is expressed in per capita terms, however, urban Thais are vastly better off than those in rural areas. Poverty is particularly pronounced in the north, northeast and far south.

Most industrial development has focussed on Bangkok, which now accounts for over 50 per cent of the nation's GDP although it has only an estimated 15 per cent of the population. Bangkok's infrastructure is straining to cope with the expansion, but despite major development schemes rural infrastructure remains inadequate to attract much business and industry away from the capital. Pollution and environmental degradation have become urgent issues in both urban and rural areas. AIDS has become the country's most pressing health issue; at least 2 million Thais are estimated to be HIV positive. Even so, Thailand's past tends to induce optimism for its future. Thai history can be seen as the story of a people with an unusual capacity for social cohesion, dissolution or evasion of conflict, and creative confrontation of unavoidable challenges.

TIMELINES

1990: Collapse of USSR and loss of foreign aid propel further economic change towards a free enterprise system

1986: Policy of 'doi moi' (renovation) adopted and overhaul of political and economic systems begins

1978: Invasion of Cambodia leads to attacks on northern borders by China

1975: RVN falls, Vietnam unified and refugees flee country

1973: Paris Peace Agreements signed

1960s: 'Vietcong' control over much of the south leads to United States increasing aid and troops are sent to support RVN

1954: Vietnam partitioned – Democratic Republic of Vietnam (DRV) in the north and Republic of Vietnam (RVN) in the south

1946-54: Indochina War between French in the south and Vietminh in the north

1859-85: French gradually acquire all of country and later establish 'French Indochina' with Cambodia and Lao

1802-20: United Vietnam under Emperor Gia Long

17th century: Country split into two clans – Trinh in the north and Nguyen in the south

11th-17th centuries: Acquires central part of the country from the Kingdom of Champa and Mekong delta from the Khmers

939: Vietnamese State re-established

618-907: The T'ang dynasty terms the country Annam – 'the pacified South'

ASEAN FOCUS GROUP

Vietnam

The Vietnamese were ruled by the Chinese for over a thousand years, from the 2nd century B.C. until the 10th century A.D. After winning their independence the Vietnamese continued looking to China as their cultural model, their prime source of concepts of government, social organisation and the arts. Culturally, Vietnam thus belonged to the 'Confucian' world of East Asia. This distinguished it sharply from neighbouring states with Theravada Buddhist or Islamic cultures. The difference in cultural outlook between Vietnam and her Southeast Asian neighbours has long contributed to conflict in the region.

But the Vietnamese regard for China also made for conflict within Vietnam itself. It proved difficult to reconcile with another Vietnamese impulse – to protect their distinctive character as a people, upholding uniquely Vietnamese cultural traditions. To adopt or to resist Chinese ideas became a perennial source of social and cultural stress within Vietnam's ruling class, and also between the ruling class and the people.

The Vietnamese state was an expanding one, intensifying such cultural stresses. The expansion – known as the 'march to the south' though it took 700 years – eased the country's population pressures and made Vietnam a major power in Southeast Asia, but it also bred deep regional differences and rivalries within Vietnamese society. 19th century Vietnam proved in poor shape to face the challenges posed by the West's political, economic and cultural expansion.

The Western impact, in the shape of French colonial rule and subsequent American intervention, aggravated the historic tensions and also cut bitter new divisions in Vietnamese society. Communism in Vietnam, as in China, won wide popular support with its promise not only of national independence but of a reintegrated and just society. As in China, communism in Vietnam now drifts uncertainly, though most observers are optimistic about Vietnam's future as a state under Communist Party control but with a free enterprise economy.

Early History

The earliest Vietnamese state occupied only the Red River Delta, today the heart of northern Vietnam. In the 2nd century B.C. this state was absorbed into the empire of Han dynasty China, the Chinese calling it Nan-yüeh or Nan-viet. Thus began over 1,000 years of Chinese rule, during which the Vietnamese became familiar with Chinese political and social institutions, the Chinese writing system and Chinese learning and arts.

They were also influenced by the Mahayana forms of Buddhism then flourishing in East Asia, another factor which would set them apart from their neighbours in Southeast Asia where Hinduism and subsequently Theravada

Buddhism flourished. Mahayana Buddhism tended to blend with Confucian and Taoist thought and, in Vietnam, with local popular religious folklore and spirit beliefs. It never developed the strong institutional networks of temples and monasteries which gave considerable political strength to Theravada Buddhism.

The high water mark of Chinese influence upon the Vietnamese was probably reached during the T'ang dynasty (61–907 A.D.), whose rulers termed the country of the Vietnamese, An-nan, or Annam – 'the pacified South'. The Vietnamese, however, never lost their sense of separate identity. In 939 A.D. they took advantage of political disorder in China to seize their independence and re-establish a Vietnamese state. In later centuries the Chinese attempted on several occasions to reassert their authority – leading to a Vietnamese perception of themselves as a permanently threatened nation – but they were successfully resisted. The early Ming did manage to take and hold Vietnam for twenty years, 1407–1428, but were ousted by forces led by one of Vietnam's greatest heroes Le Loi, founder of the Le dynasty, 1428–1789.

The history of Vietnam after independence in the 10th century would be marked by two principal, and conflict-provoking, tendencies. Firstly, the development of a Confucian state and high culture modelled on China. By the 15th century, Vietnam had a system of government similar in all but size to that of its mighty northern neighbour. The Vietnamese emperor, at the capital Hanoi, presided over a mandarin bureaucracy educated in the Confucian classics. Law, administrative structures, literature and the arts all followed Chinese forms. The educated class also tended to prefer to use Chinese rather than the Vietnamese language. In theory the adoption of the Confucian model of social organisation should have conferred enlightened government on Vietnam. In practice it produced a ruling class culturally alienated from their subjects. This problem was compounded by the grip on the country's commercial life maintained by Chinese merchants allied with the Vietnamese ruling class.

Nevertheless, popular Vietnamese culture absorbed many attitudes and values of Chinese derivation, through acceptance of codes of law and morality promulgated by government and spread by scholars. Thus ordinary Vietnamese displayed such characteristically 'Confucian' traits as respect for hierarchy, emphasis on an individual's social obligations, intense family loyalty and reverence for education and scholarship. Even so, Vietnamese popular culture always remained self-consciously distinct, hostile to China and wary of the country's Sinophile upper class.

The second main tendency in the history of Vietnam after gaining independence from China was southward expansion, and this would compound the cultural tensions. Military in organisation, the expansion was driven basically by the need to find farming land for a growing population. Between the 11th and 17th centuries it gradually extinguished the kingdom of Champa, in what is today central Vietnam. It then took the Mekong Delta from the Khmers, and during the

19th century would probably have overwhelmed the whole of Cambodia, had not the Thais challenged the Vietnamese advance and the French brought it to a halt by establishing a 'protectorate' over Cambodia in 1863. One can see here some of the seeds which have led to anti-Vietnamese feelings in Cambodia which are strongly sown today by the Khmer Rouge.

The 'march to the south' allowed rival power blocs to develop within Vietnamese society. The 16th century saw intermittent civil war in Vietnam. In the 17th century the country was split between two powerful clans, the Trinh in the north and the Nguyen in the south. The frontier established between them was only a few kilometres from the site of the demilitarised zone which would separate North and South Vietnam between 1954 and 1975. In the 17th and 18th centuries the Nguyen rulers in the south became responsible for the country's continued expansion.

The cultural differences between northerners and southerners popularly recognised in modern Vietnam may have their origins in the 'march to the south'. The circumstances of the 'frontier' southerners contrasted with those of 'stay-at-home' northerners. In the south settler families were thrown on their own resources, in a tropical environment unlike that of the temperate north. Deference towards officialdom declined. Village organisation of economic and administrative matters – elaborate in the north – also declined in the south. On the southern frontier facilities for the reinforcement of Confucian culture were virtually non-existent.

At the same time the southern settlers were encountering alternative ideas, particularly religious concepts, in the cultures of the Chams and Khmers and also upland tribal (or montagnard) groups. Here, perhaps, were the beginnings of the cultural dichotomies popularly perceived today. Northerners are noted for their conservatism, deference to the group, reserved manners and respect for the intellectual life; southerners for their outgoing approach to life, free-wheeling attitudes toward authority, outspoken manners and eclectic religious life.

Whatever the developing differences the Vietnamese perception of themselves as basically one people remained unquestioned. This was dramatically demonstrated in the Tay Son Rebellion which broke out in Vietnam in 1771. A vast 'revolution from below', the rebellion swept away the Nguyen and Trinh regimes which had divided Vietnam, and also the long since nominal Le imperial dynasty.

The rebels also repelled a Chinese invasion, and turned on Chinese merchants in Vietnam. They faltered only when faced with the task of practical government. A member of the southern Nguyen clan, Nguyen Anh, raised forces and by 1802 managed to subdue the rebel forces. He became the emperor Gia Long, first of Vietnam's Nguyen emperors and the first ruler to preside over a united Vietnam for more than two centuries.

The 19th century Confucian revival

Emperor from 1802 to 1820, Gia Long recognised what an administrative and defence nightmare Vietnam's geography had become by the early 19th century – two fertile deltas 1,000 kilometres apart, connected by a narrow coastal corridor. Ignoring Hanoi (and thus incurring northerner resentment) he established his capital in the centre of the country at Hué. There he built a palace complex that was a scaled down replica of Peking's Forbidden City. The symbolism was appropriate – Gia Long and his son Minh Mang (emperor 1820 –1841) would attempt to establish in Vietnam the most thorough copy yet seen of Chinese administrative concepts and methods. Honourably intentioned, the attempt would prove a disaster.

From the 1830s onwards rebellion flared frequently in protest at the level of bureaucratic intervention in daily life, the rigidities and absurdities of mandarinal decrees and, above all, at the level of taxation demanded by the system. The renewed concern with Confucian models also diminished the ability of the Nguyen imperial government to deal realistically with the growing challenges from the West. Some members of the Vietnamese scholar class recognised the need to study the West, but they were in the minority. Disastrously, Emperor Minh Mang and his successors (Thieu Tri, emperor 1841–1847, and Tu Duc, emperor 1847–1883) chose to confront and repress the religion of the West, Christianity.

French Catholic missionaries had been active in Vietnam since the mid-17th century. They had helped Gia Long defeat the Tay Son rebels and establish his imperial dynasty, assisting him with men and resources. By the mid-19th century there were an estimated 450,000 Catholic converts in Vietnam. Vietnamese government had always been wary of organised religion in any form, as a potential threat to Confucian authority, and now Christianity seemed a serious challenge. In successive campaigns of repression, thousands of Christians and their priests were killed and Christian villages were levelled. The persecutions shocked Catholics in France, and unwittingly provided a pretext for French intervention in Vietnam.

Colonial history

In 1859 a French naval expedition seized Saigon, following an unsuccessful attempt on the then more significant port of Da Nang, which was close to Hué. Emperor Tu Duc faced rebellion in the north and in 1862 conceded to the French, who gained by treaty, Saigon and its three surrounding provinces. In 1869 the French seized three further adjoining provinces, thus completing the territory of the colony they would call Cochin China.

The French conquered the remainder of Vietnam between 1883 and 1885, in the course of a complicated conflict in the country's north. The north had collapsed in chaos fomented by both Vietnamese and expatriate Chinese rebels. The Vietnamese imperial government had lost all capacity to control events. Both China and France regarded Vietnam as their 'sphere of influence' and sent forces; the French eventually repelling the Chinese.

The French then declared 'protectorates' over northern Vietnam (Tonkin) and central Vietnam (Annam), where they would retain a line of 'puppet' Nguyen emperors until Bao Dai, emperor 1926–1945 and later nominal 'chief of state' from 1949 to 1956. In 1885 some Vietnamese mandarins, outraged at the French intrusion, organised a resistance movement called Can Vuong ('Aid the King'), which would persist for several years, but after its pacification the French would rule relatively securely until 1940.

French colonial rule would bring many elements of modernity to the country, amongst them handsome cities, sewered and lit by electricity, the Saigon-Hanoi railway, modern port facilities, a network of metalled roads, and modern education and medicine for those – a small minority – who could afford them. The French also vastly expanded Vietnam's rice output and linked Vietnam into the world economy on the basis of exports of rice and, to a lesser extent, rubber and other products. Colonialism's most significant impact, however, was to increase divisiveness in Vietnam – administratively, economically and socially.

Administratively, 'Vietnam' disappeared off the map, outraging Vietnamese nationalists and enhancing regionalist tendencies, the country being divided into Cochin China (administrative centre Saigon), Annam (Hué) and Tonkin (Hanoi). The three segments became parts of 'French Indochina' along with Cambodia and Lao. Differing approaches to administration north and south also enhanced regionalism. Cochin China, constitutionally a French colony, experienced French administrators and French legal forms. Saigon became the leading and most westernised city of Indochina, an alluring showpiece of modern fashions and culture. In the 'protectorates' Tonkin and Annam, by contrast, the French endeavoured to retain indigenous administrative and legal systems, if only for the sake of cheapness. Hanoi and Hué remained much quieter places than Saigon.

Colonial economic policies also pulled the country apart, though the fundamental reasons for this lay in the circumstances inherited by the French. In Vietnam's north the French found a ready-made economic crisis – a densely crowded population dependent on subsistence rice agriculture. By 1929 the average population density in the Tonkin Delta countryside would be 975 per square kilometre. Most families held inadequately small plots and were in debt; the whole system depended on an elaborate but ancient and dilapidated complex of irrigation dykes.

The French were unwilling to industrialise in Vietnam – industry was for metropolitan France, not for her colonies – and thus had no fundamental answers to these problems. By the 1930s only about 120,000 people were classified as industrial workers in Vietnam, many of these being miners in the north's coal, zinc and tin mines. Some northerners moved to the south's rubber plantations as indentured labour, often in scandalously exploitative conditions, but this labour traffic had little impact on the north's basic economic problems.

In contrast, Cochin China was the success story of French colonialism. When French rule began the Mekong Delta was still relatively lightly populated. Much delta land was still unharnessed swamp. From the 1870s water control and irrigation programs made available vast new areas of farming land. Later the French would boast that they had boosted Vietnam's rice lands by 420 per cent. The development of the Mekong Delta enabled Vietnam to become by the 1920s one of the world's leading rice exporters, although the absolute primacy of rice – accounting for over 70 per cent of colonial Vietnam's exports – made the economy a precariously unbalanced one. It was also debatable, ironically, whether the southern farmers were much better off than their northern cousins. Most southerners became sharecroppers on the vast estates created out of the reclaimed lands; as such they enjoyed little security or prosperity.

Vietnamese histories recall, with horror, French taxation policies, claiming that the Vietnamese were the most highly taxed people in the colonial world. That is debatable, but French defence, administrative and public works costs were high and so therefore were their taxes. The promotion of a government opium monopoly, as late as the 1930s, is remembered with particular distaste. Other imposts included a poll tax and taxes on alcohol and salt.

Culture and politics in colonial Vietnam

Socially and culturally, colonial Vietnam was a place of ferment. The collapse of Confucian government and the triumph of the 'barbarian' West had thrown all traditional Vietnamese beliefs and values into question. The Vietnamese upper and middle classes were small in numbers, but they pursued modern (as against Confucian) education avidly, and more than made up for their small numbers with the intensity of their debates on the way forward for Vietnam.

Here too divisiveness grew. Some opted for various Western models of thought and behaviour. Others looked to China for ways of reconstructing a shattered Confucian world (but found only conflict there too). Still others looked to Japan. By the 1920s, however, the Vietnamese intelligentsia reached consensus on the adoption of *quoc ngu*, a relatively simple Romanised written form of Vietnamese invented by French missionaries, in preference to the traditional but cumbersome Chinese-style characters (Chu Nom). *Quoc ngu* helped the growth of an impressive modern Vietnamese literary culture, and the production of popularly accessible newspapers and political literature.

Even so, Vietnamese political enthusiasts made little popular headway before World War II. The moderates of the Constitutionalist Party, who favoured gradual development of democratic structures, were considered too pro-French by most

Vietnamese, and in any case the French were dismissive of their plans.

Some radical-thinking Vietnamese established in 1927 a party imitating China's Kuomintang, the VNQDD (Viet Nam Quoc Dan Dang). However their numbers were decimated following an abortive uprising in 1930. In the same year some young Vietnamese attracted to Marx and Lenin founded the Indochina Communist Party (ICP), but they also became targets of French surveillance and unusually severe repression, although they were able to operate semi-openly in Cochin China during the Popular Front era in French government, between 1936 and 1939. They were embarrassed, however, by the policy twists and turns in their orders from Stalin's Comintern, and many Vietnamese left-wingers turned to Trotskyism. The extent of either Marxist group's popular appeal in Vietnam in the 1930s is debatable. The ICP's achievements before World War II are probably exaggerated by modern official histories, though certainly not the courage and determination of its pioneer members.

In Vietnam the most imposing popular movements before World War II, in terms of numbers, were in fact religious movements. Cao Dai, a sect founded in the south in 1925 and claiming to harmonise the East and the West and unique Vietnamese traditions, had over 1 million adherents by the late 1930s.

A Buddhist sect, *Hoa Hao*, was also attracting large numbers in the south by that time. Christianity had also grown in Vietnam, by the 1930s claiming around 10 per cent of the population (then about 30 million). These and other flourishing religious movements would pose problems for Vietnamese nationalism after World War II.

World War II and the First Indochina War, 1940–1954

Japanese forces entered French Indochina in 1940 and quickly reached an agreement with the colonial government similar to that reached in France between Japan's ally Nazi Germany and the Vichy regime. Thus French colonial authority survived – but only until March 1945, when the Japanese interned all French in Indochina. The Japanese then set up a nominal Vietnamese government under the emperor Bao Dai and other dignitaries.

By early 1945 Vietnam was sliding towards chaos. The wartime disruptions to the economy, Japanese seizures of rice and other goods, plus disastrous weather which wrecked two successive harvests combined to produce famine in Tonkin and Annam. The famine's death toll possibly exceeded 1 million when war ended precipitously on 15th August, producing effectively a power vacuum in Vietnam. The stage was set for the 'August Revolution' of the Vietminh.

The Vietminh (Viet Nam Doc Lap Dong Minh: League for the Independence of Vietnam) had been set up in 1941 as a front organisation of the ICP, whose leadership was then gathered at Pac Bo, an isolated spot high in the mountains on the Sino-Vietnamese border. Here they had been joined by Ho Chi Minh, now in his fifties and back in Vietnam for the first time since 1911, although as Comintern agent for Southeast Asia in the late 1920s and 1930s he had maintained intermittent contact with Vietnam's communists. Henceforth, Ho would be free of control from Moscow and in Vietnam would cut his own revolutionary path, though he would always try to maintain good relations with both Soviet and Chinese communists, if only for the aid they might offer him. In Vietnam Ho would prove to be a brilliant if devious revolutionary tactician, a skilled leader of the many talented young Vietnamese attracted to communism, and also a hugely popular political leader, speaking and writing in terms that moved and exhilarated large numbers of his countrymen and women.

During the war the Vietminh developed a strategy for its cadres and guerrilla forces to seize power at the war's end, when Vietnam could expect to be in disarray – as indeed happened. Within days of the Japanese surrender Vietminh forces (under the banner of national independence rather than socialism) took control of most of northern and central Vietnam. They were less successful in the south where Vietminh organisers were recognised as ICP members and found themselves opposed by political, business and religious forces. Nevertheless on September 2nd in Hanoi, Ho Chi Minh declared Vietnam's reunification and independence.

Vietnam's fate was to remain divided, however. In the north the Allies had appointed Chinese nationalist forces to relieve the Japanese. The Chinese occupied the north until May 1946, and, crucially, left the French there interned while tolerating Ho Chi Minh's government, thus enabling it to consolidate its power. By contrast, in southern Vietnam the Japanese were relieved by British Indian troops.

Their commander, dismayed at the political mayhem in Saigon, released and rearmed the French. By late 1945 French forces again controlled southern Vietnam. During 1946 Ho's government anxiously negotiated with the French, buying time as both sides prepared for war, which finally broke out in December 1946.

The French, fighting a conventional war, appeared by early 1947 to have all strategic positions in Vietnam under their control. The Vietminh, however, had settled down to an underground 'people's war', organising and educating the population to support a possibly long guerrilla campaign. The war's turning point came in 1950, when first the new communist government of China and then the USSR began to assist the Vietminh with arms and other material. International communist support for the Vietminh precipitated direct United States aid for the French war effort, but by the early 1950s the French were beginning to weary of the inconclusive conflict. The fall of the French garrison at Dien Bien Phu in May 1954 – a brilliant victory for the Vietminh's military strategist Vo Nguyen Giap – effectively signalled the end of France's attempt to hold Vietnam.

Vietnam Partitioned and the Vietnam War, 1954–1975

As Dien Bien Phu fell, the great powers were meeting at Geneva to seek a settlement of the war. The result was a ceasefire and partition of Vietnam at the 17th parallel. The North, to be known as the Democratic Republic of Vietnam (DRV), would be governed by Ho Chi Minh and his group, who since 1950 had emerged as unequivocal communists, dedicated not only to national independence but to socialist revolution. The South would be headed by Bao Dai, who had abdicated as emperor in 1945 but became nominal 'chief of state' under the French in 1949. Ho's victorious forces settled for partition presumably because the Geneva conference had also heralded elections in 1956, to establish government for a reunited Vietnam. As national heroes they were confident of winning such elections.

The elections never took place. France withdrew from Vietnam and the United States backed Ngo Dinh Diem, a Catholic and staunch anti-communist, as Prime Minister under Bao Dai. With American aid, Diem suppressed or bought off rival southern anti-communist leaders and their disparate followings. In 1955 Diem won a referendum to determine whether he or Bao Dai should head the South. Bao Dai left Vietnam and Diem declared himself President of the Republic of Vietnam (RVN). With American support Diem refused to discuss the proposed nationwide elections.

In the North the DRV government, appealing to long-cherished community values, pressed ahead with socialisation, including collectivisation of agriculture. Those deemed 'capitalists' and 'rich peasants' suffered, sometimes brutally, but the majority poor seem to have accepted socialism's promises. Popular support for Ho Chi Minh's government remained enormously high.

By contrast Diem was never to be genuinely popular in the politically and religiously fragmented South, except perhaps amongst his fellow Catholics (almost 1 million northern Catholics were shipped south by the U.S. navy in 1954). Diem, as indifferent to economics as he was to democracy, offered little hope to the southern poor, and spent most of his U.S. aid on his security forces, which were under the command of his brother Ngo Dinh Nhu. Other members of his avaricious family also provoked resentment.

In 1959 the DRV government, observing the build-up of popular opposition towards Diem the 'American puppet', sponsored a new Vietminh-style front organisation for the South. This was the NLF (National Liberation Front – called 'Vietcong' by its opponents). Coy about its degree of control by communists, the NLF appealed to Vietnamese patriotism and morality, promising to oust American influence and to set up fair and honest government.

By the early 1960s NLF guerrilla forces were in command of wide areas of the southern countryside, and had won sympathisers at all levels of society. Alarmed, United States President Kennedy stepped up aid to Diem and sent

American military 'advisers' – 17,500 by 1963. By mid-1963, however, Diem and his brother Nhu had antagonised almost every sector of Southern society. The world was startled when Buddhist monks began burning themselves to death in protest against the regime. Plotters within South Vietnam's military concluded that Diem and Nhu had to go, and in October 1963 they were murdered.

Four years of unstable government would follow in South Vietnam, until in 1967 General Nguyen Van Thieu would emerge as President. A skillful manipulator of the vast patronage which American aid made possible, Thieu would remain President until 1975. But meanwhile in the United States Kennedy's successor Johnson had decided to confront the NLF directly with United States power. In early 1965 the United States Air Force began bombing targets in both South and North Vietnam and United States ground troops landed in the South. What came to be called 'the Vietnam War' was now unequivocally under way.

A process of 'escalation' followed: China, the USSR and the Eastern Bloc raised their aid to the DRV, which raised its commitment of material and men to the NLF. In turn, the United States raised the stakes further, to a peak of 525,000 troops by 1967. The United States received some support from Australia, New Zealand and some anti-communist Asian governments, but its major allies stayed aloof from the conflict.

In 1968 at Tet, the lunar new year, NLF/DRV forces launched a massive offensive throughout the South. The offensive was repelled, but its strength shocked both the Johnson administration and the American public, which had been led to believe that the war was being won.

Richard Nixon, elected President in 1968, and his special adviser Henry Kissinger, had to find alternative strategies to 'escalation'. They pursued 'Vietnamisation' of the war, reducing United States troop levels and encouraging the South with ever-increasing aid to increase its levels. By 1973 the South's armed forces numbered over one million; half the South's men between the ages of 18 and 35 were in the armed forces.

The Nixon/Kissinger strategies also included increased aerial warfare. American bombing of both North and South and also of Cambodia wreaked social, economic and ecological devastation. By the war's end 60 per cent of southern villages would be destroyed or rendered unsafe; only 35 per cent of an essentially peasant population would still live in rural areas. However the bombing never proved decisive to the course of the war. It even failed to interdict the legendary Ho Chi Minh Trail, the network of mountainous trails down which the DRV supplied its war effort in the South. Some American opinion consistently urged the expansion of the ground war into the North, but neither Johnson nor Nixon were ever willing to take that course, fearing that it might precipitate full scale American confrontation with the USSR and China – the dreaded World War III. Thus the DRV, despite the bombing, always remained a secure base for the DRV/NLF war effort in the South.

Meanwhile, Nixon and Kissinger also pursued diplomacy. Talks between United States and DRV/NLF representatives had begun in Paris in 1968. For years they dragged on inconclusively, but in January 1973 the 'Paris Peace Agreements' were signed by the United States, the Saigon government (reluctantly, under intense United States pressure), the DRV and the PRG (the Provisional Revolutionary Government of the NLF).

Crucially for the DRV/NLF, the first article of the agreements recognised the 'independence, sovereignty, unity and territorial integrity' of Vietnam. Other articles called for a ceasefire, at which point the contending Vietnamese forces could claim whatever territory they held in the South, pending elections to determine the South's future government. The agreements also called for the total withdrawal of United States troops and military personnel within 60 days. This article proved in fact to be the only one of the Paris agreements which was fully carried out. The American boys went home, but in South Vietnam war continued unabated.

The morale of the Southern forces began to slide, particularly after Nixon's resignation in August 1974 over the Watergate scandal. His successor as President, Gerald Ford, had little influence over a Congress now disillusioned with the war and reluctant to sustain United States aid to the Saigon regime. In contrast, the DRV/NLF forces, legitimately ensconced in the South under the Paris agreements, were increasingly confident that victory was in sight. Guerrilla war had long since given way to conventional military tactics. By now the amount and sophisticated nature of their weaponry, supplied by their allies, matched that of the Southern forces.

Even so, the speed with which the war ended stunned both sides. DRV/NLF forces launched a limited offensive in the South's central highlands in mid-March 1975. RVN forces panicked when ordered to retreat, creating a country-wide rout which was slowed by Southern detachments in only a handful of places. The Southern government collapsed, and DRV/NLF forces entered Saigon on 30th April. The last Americans remaining in South Vietnam had been evacuated just hours before, along with some leading Southerners closely identified with the American presence.

Vietnam Since 1975

The major question in April 1975 concerned the speed with which Vietnam would be reintegrated. Since the 1950s the historic differences between north and south had been hugely magnified. The northerners had existed under an austere, disciplined socialism which re-emphasised their traditional regard for social hierarchy and community obligation. The southerners had been introduced to a quasi-capitalist consumer economy, sustained by American aid, and to the trappings of American popular culture.

In 1975 the victorious DRV government revealed a profound distrust of even pro-communist southerners, and moved swiftly to subordinate the south. The NLF and its provisional government were disbanded, and administrative control was imposed directly from Hanoi. In 1976 the country was renamed the Socialist Republic of Vietnam (SRV), though in practice it was a 'greater DRV', dominated by northerners. In the same year plans for the collectivisation of southern agriculture were announced; socialisation of the south's entire economy, integrating it with the northern economy, proceeded swiftly over the next two years.

Heady from their military triumphs perhaps, Vietnam's leaders envisaged equally dramatic results from their decisive action in the economic sphere. Instead they engendered acute economic crisis, made worse by flood and other natural disasters in 1977 and 1978. Ambitious industrial targets failed to be achieved; most seriously, rice and other agricultural outputs plummeted and food rations had to be slashed.

In late 1978 Vietnam invaded Cambodia and ousted the socialist genocidal and virulently anti-Vietnamese Pol Pot regime. In retaliation China attacked Vietnam's northern frontier zone. Traditional regional antagonisms and rivalries had quickly reasserted themselves over the apparent international socialist comradeship of the years before 1975. In Vietnam these hostilities exacerbated the domestic crisis. In the early 1980s many Chinese and Sino-Vietnamese fled Vietnam, either to China or as 'boat people' to overseas countries, sharply boosting the statistics on people fleeing Vietnam since 1975.

The scale of the economic crisis forced some softening of policy as early as 1979, but hardline neo-Stalinist opinion essentially prevailed within Vietnam's ruling group until 1985, when Gorbachev's reforms in the USSR heartened reformers in Vietnam. In 1986 the Sixth National Congress of the Vietnam Communist Party formally approved the policy of *doi moi*, or renovation.

Politically, *doi moi* has meant the emergence of a new, younger leadership, the streamlining (relatively) of the country's administrative apparatus, reforms in the Party's structure, and moves towards the rule of law, answerable government and greater freedom of expression. Economic change has gone much further than political reform, propelled by the collapse of the Soviet Union and the Eastern Bloc's abandonment of socialism, which in practical terms has meant the loss to Vietnam of aid which accounted for up to 30 per cent of the state budget.

China's example has also been a major if unacknowledged factor in determining Vietnamese policy. Like China, Vietnam is now a hybrid, a state under one-party control, in theory socialist, but with a booming free enterprise economy alongside faltering state enterprises.

As with China some analysts question the long term stability of such a system. Free enterprise economic activity is perhaps intrinsically pluralist. In Vietnam the historically more pluralist south has shot ahead of the north economically since *doi moi*. Some are worried the country's pull-apart tendencies could re-emerge. On the other hand, Vietnam's current rulers are firmly in command as the rightful heirs of the socialist patriots who overcame France and the United States and reunited the fatherland.

The challenge they face is not at present to their power, but to their capacity to persist with *doi moi*, to see through the myriad social and cultural, as well as economic and political, changes demanded by *doi moi*, and in the process to maintain stability in a country where stability has rarely been experienced.

Further Reading

GENERAL

Osborne, Milton — *Southeast Asia. An Introductory Illustrated History*, 6th edition, Sydney: Allen & Unwin, 1995.

Reid, Anthony — *Southeast Asia in the Age of Commerce, 1450-1680*, New Haven: Yale University Press, 1988

Reid, Anthony — *Southeast Asia in the Early Modern Era: Trade, Power and Belief*, Ithaca NY: Cornell University Press, 1993.

Steinberg, David J (ed) — *In Search of Southeast Asia*, Sydney: Allen & Unwin, 1987.

BRUNEI

Ranjit Singh, D S — *Brunei 1834-1983. The Problems of Political Survival*, Singapore: Oxford University Press, 1984.

Turnbull, C Mary — *A History of Malaysia, Singapore and Brunei*, Sydney: Allen & Unwin, 1989.

CAMBODIA

Chandler, David — *A History of Cambodia*, 2nd edition, Boulder, Co.: Westview Press & Sydney: Allen & Unwin, 1992.

Kiernan, Ben — *How Pol Pot Came to Power*, London: Verso, 1985.

Osborne, Milton — *Sihanouk: Prince of Light, Prince of Darkness*, Sydney: Allen & Unwin, 1994.

Ross, Russell R (ed) — *Cambodia: A Country Study*, Washington D.C.: Library of Congress Federal Research Division, 1990.

INDONESIA

Booth, Anne (ed) — *The Oil Boom and After. Indonesian Economic Policy and Performance in the Soeharto Era*, Singapore: Oxford University Press, 1992.

Legge, J D	*Sukarno. A Political Biography*, Sydney: Allen & Unwin, 1985.
MacIntyre, Andrew	*Indonesia*, Sydney: The Asia-Australia Institute, University of New South Wales, 1993.
MacIntyre, Andrew	*Business and Politics in Indonesia*, Sydney: Allen & Unwin, 1990.
Ricklefs, M C	*A History of Modern Indonesia Since c. 1300*, London: Macmillan, 1993.
Vatikiotis, Michael	*Indonesian Politics Under Suharto*, London: Routledge, 1993.

LAO

Brown, MacAlister & Zasloff, Joseph J	*Apprentice Revolutionaries: The Communist Movement in Laos, 1930-1985*, Stanford, Calif: Hoover Institution Press, 1986.
Dommen, Arthur J	*Laos: Keystone of Indochina*, Boulder, Co.: Westview Press, 1985.
Stuart-Fox, Martin & Kooyman, Mary	*Historical Dictionary of Laos*, Metuchen, NJ: Scarecrow Press, 1992.

MALAYSIA

Andaya, Barbara & Leonard	*A History of Malaysia*, London: Macmillan, 1982.
Black, Ian	*Malaysia*, Sydney: The Asia-Australia Institute, University of New South Wales, 1993.
Kaur, Amarjit	*Historical Dictionary of Malaysia,* Metuchen, N J: Scarecrow Press, 1993.
Means, Gordon P	*Malaysian Politics: The Second Generation*, Singapore & New York: Oxford University Press, 1991.
Mohamad, Mahathir bin	*The Malay Dilemma*, Singapore: Times Books International, 1970.

MYANMAR

Aung-Thwin, M	*Pagan: The Origins of Modern Burma,* Honolulu: University of Hawaii Press, 1985.
Badgley, John	'Myanmar in 1993: A Watershed Year', *Asian Survey,* 34: 2: February 1994: 153-59.
Lintner, Bertil	'Outrage: Burma's Struggle For Democracy', *Far Eastern Economic Review,* Hong Kong, 1990.
Osborne, Milton	*Burma,* Sydney: University of New South Wales, Asia-Australia Institute, University of New South Wales, 1994.
Silverstein, Josef (ed)	*Independent Burma at Forty Years: Six Assessments,* Ithaca: Cornell Southeast Asia Program, 1989.
Smith, Martin	*Burma: Insurgency and the Politics of Ethnicity,* London: 1991.
Taylor, Robert	*The State in Burma,* Honolulu: University of Hawaii Press, 1988.

PHILIPPINES

Friend, Theodore	*The Blue-Eyed Enemy. Japan Against the West in Java and Luzon, 1942-1945,* Princeton: Princeton University Press, 1988.
Hawes, Gary	'Marcos, His Cronies, and the Philippines Failure to Develop', in Ruth T McVey, *Southeast Asian Capitalists,* Ithaca, NY: Cornell University, 1992, 145-60.
Ileto, Reynaldo	*Pasyon and Revolution. Popular Movements in the Philippines, 1840-1910,* Manila: Ateneo de Manila Press, 1979.
McCoy, Alfred W & d Jesus, C (eds)	*Philippine Social History,* Sydney: Allen & Unwin, 1982.
McCoy, Alfred W (ed)	*Southeast Asia Under Japanese Occupation,* New Haven: Yale University Southeast Asian Studies, 1980.

Paredes, Ruby R (ed)	*Philippine Colonial Democracy*, New Haven: Yale University Southeast Asian Studies, 1988.
Pinches, Michael	'The Philippines: The Regional Exception', *The Pacific Review*, 5: 4: 1992: 390-401.
Reidinger, Jeffrey	'The Philippines in 1993', *Asian Survey*, 34: 2: February 1994: 139-52.

SINGAPORE

Carnegie, Georgina & Sharpe, Diana	*Singapore*, Sydney: The Asia-Australia Institute, University of New South Wales, 1993.
Minchen, James	*No Man is an Island. A Portrait of Singapore's Lee Kuan Yew*, Sydney: Allen & Unwin, 1990.
Rodan, Garry	*The Political Economy of Singapore's Industrialization: National State and International Capital,* Basingstoke: Macmillan, 1989.
Siddique, S & Sholam, N	*Singapore's Little India*, Singapore: Institute of Southeast Asian Studies, 1982.
Turnbull, C M	*A History of Singapore, 1819-1988*, Singapore: Oxford University Press, 1992.

THAILAND

Akira, Suehiro	*Capital Accumulation in Thailand, 1855-1985*, Tokyo: The Centre for East Asian Cultural Studies, 1989.
Hewison, Kevin	*Politics and Power in Thailand: Essays in Political Economy*, Journal of Contemporary Asia Publishers, Manila, 1989.
Wright Jr, Joseph J	*The Balancing Act: A History of Modern Thailand*, Bangkok: Asia Books, 1991.
Wyatt, David K	*Thailand. A Short History*, New Haven: Yale University Press, 1984.

VIETNAM

Duiker, William J	*Historical Dictionary of Vietnam*, Metuchen, N J: Scarecrow Press, 1989.
Jamieson, Neil	*Understanding Vietnam*, Berkeley: University of California, 1993.

Karnow, Stanley	*Vietnam. A History*, London: Penguin, 1984.
Kolko, Gabriel	*Vietnam. Anatomy of War 1940-1975*, London: Allen & Unwin, 1986.
Lockhart, Greg	*Nation in Arms*, Sydney: Allen & Unwin, 1989.
Porter, Gareth	*Vietnam: The Politics of Bureaucratic Socialism*, Ithaca NY: Cornell University Press, 1993.
Turley, William S	*The Second Indochina War: A Short Political and Military History*, Boulder, Co.: Westview Press, 1986.

Cambodia

Indonesia

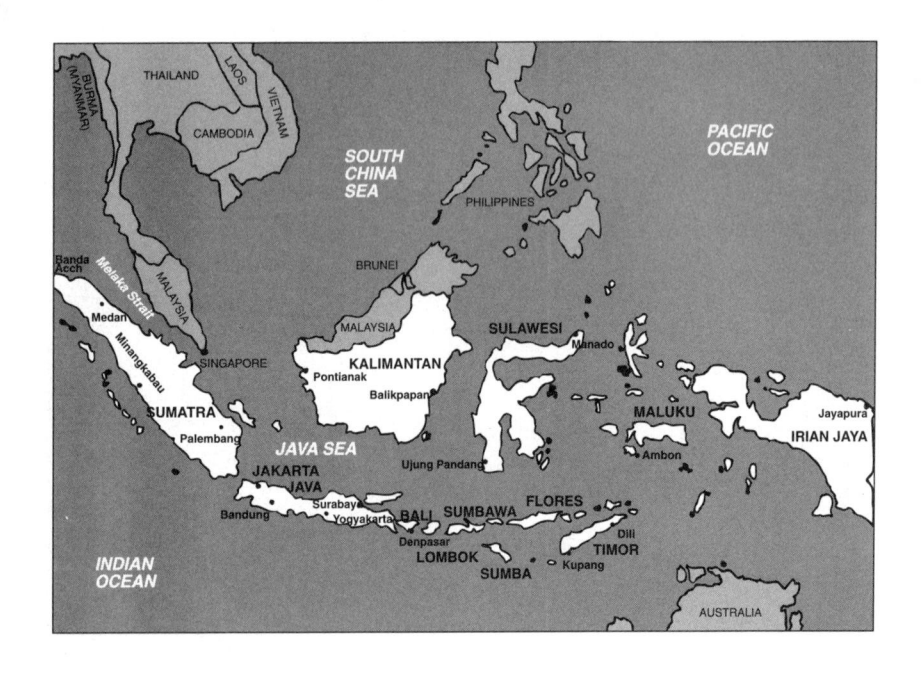

ASEAN FOCUS GROUP

Lao PDR

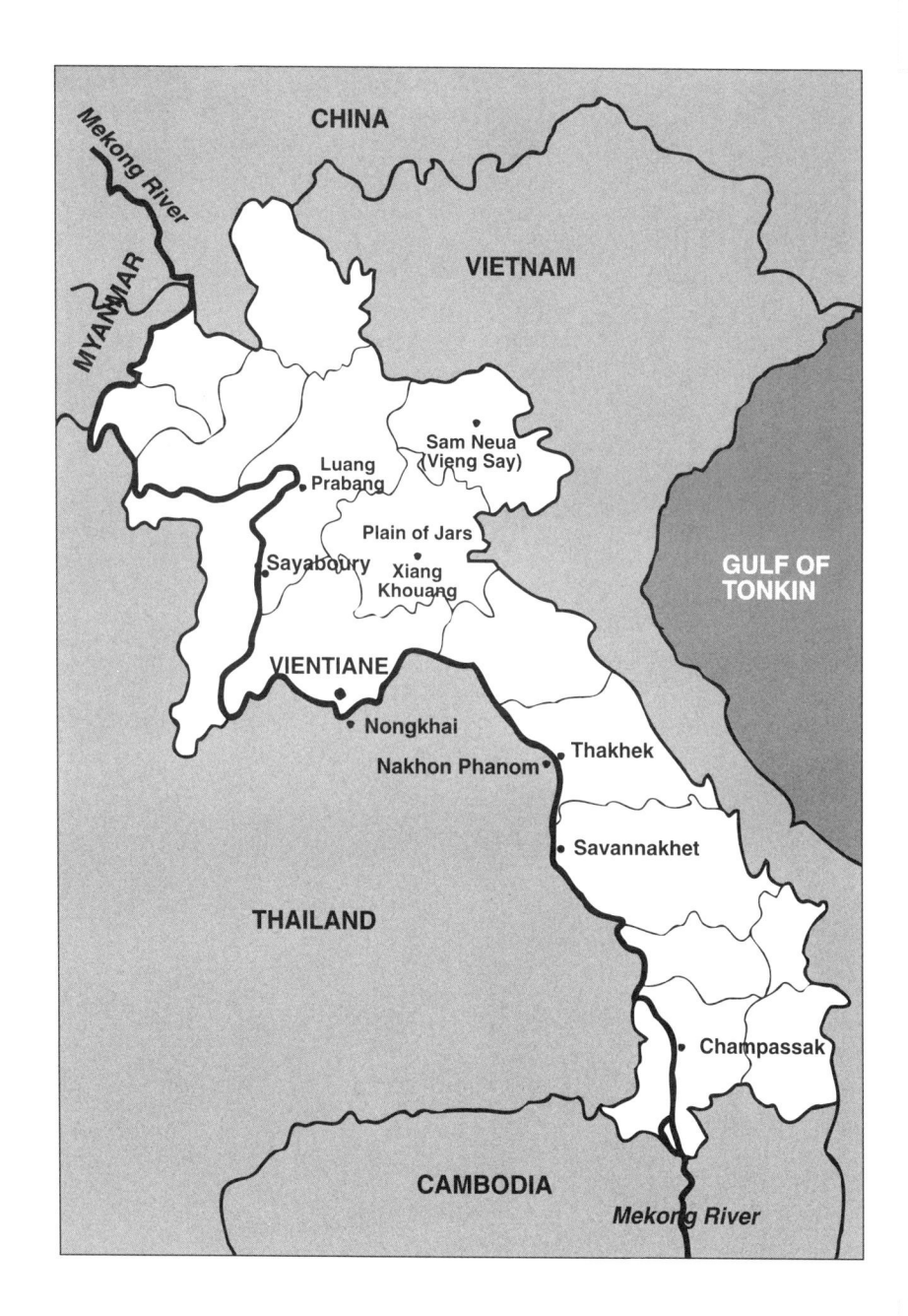

Peninsular Malaysia

East Malaysia

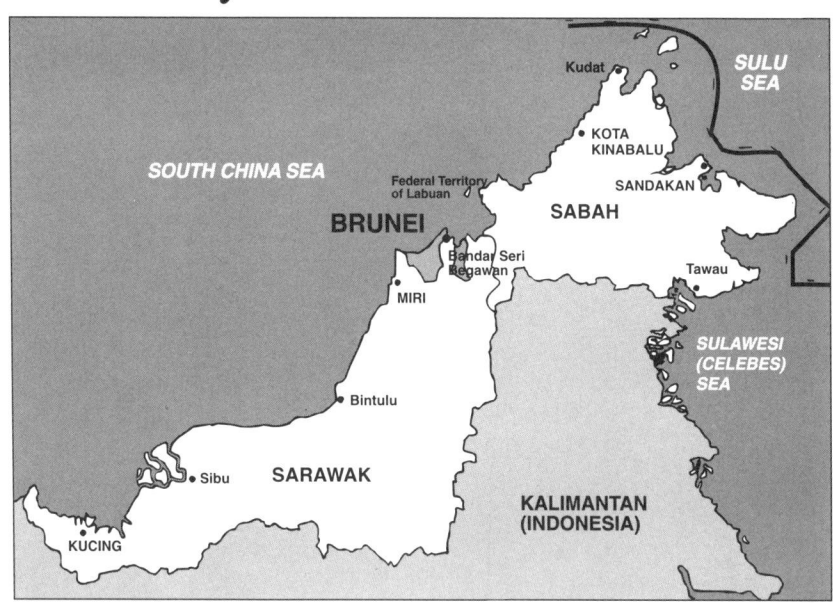

Brunei

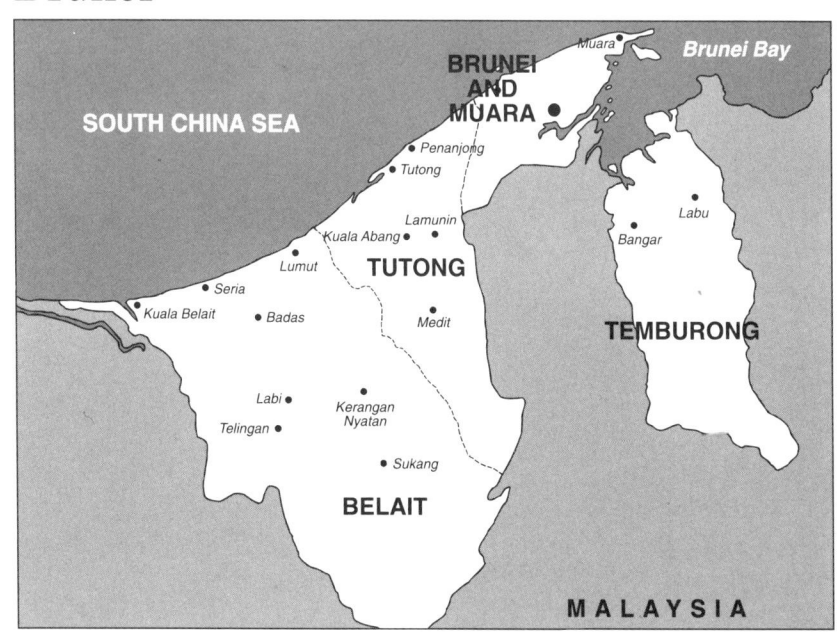

Myanmar

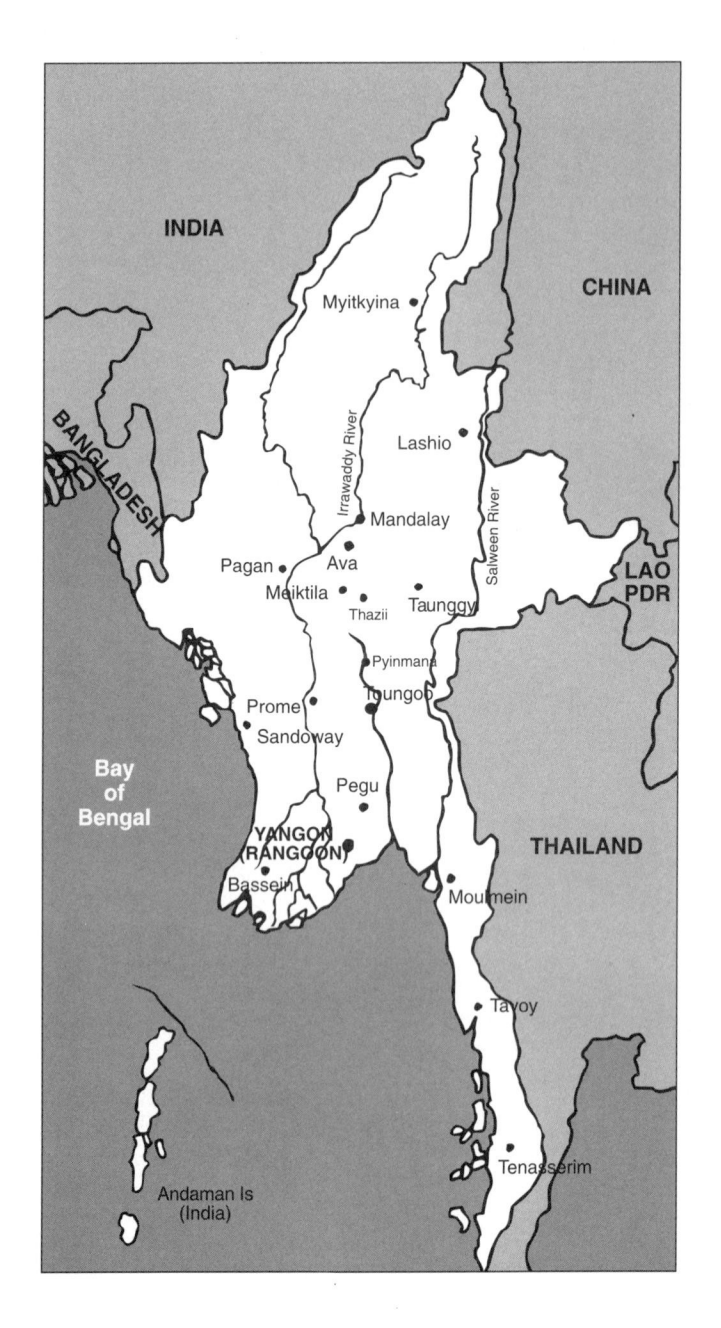

ASEAN FOCUS GROUP

Philippines

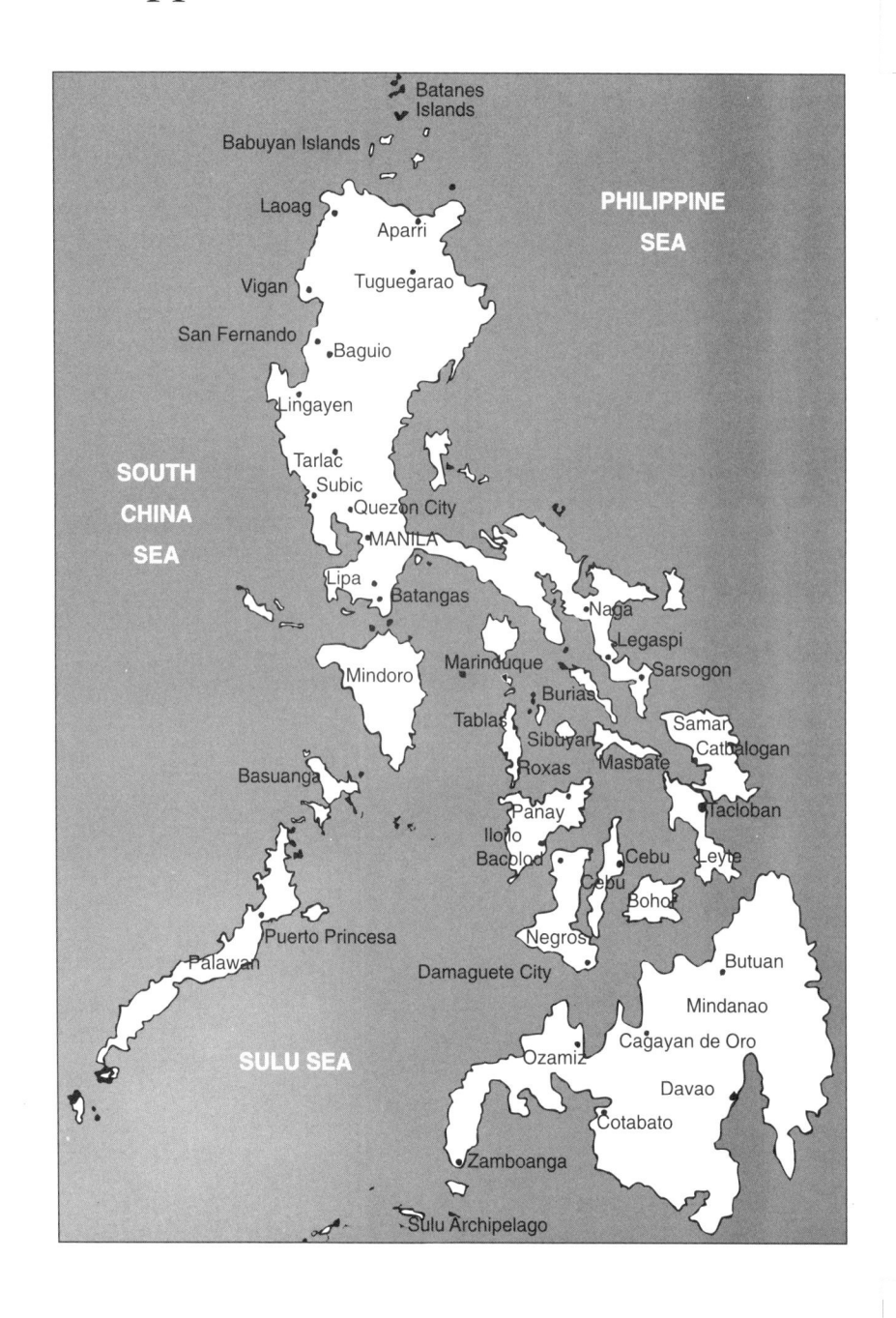

Singapore

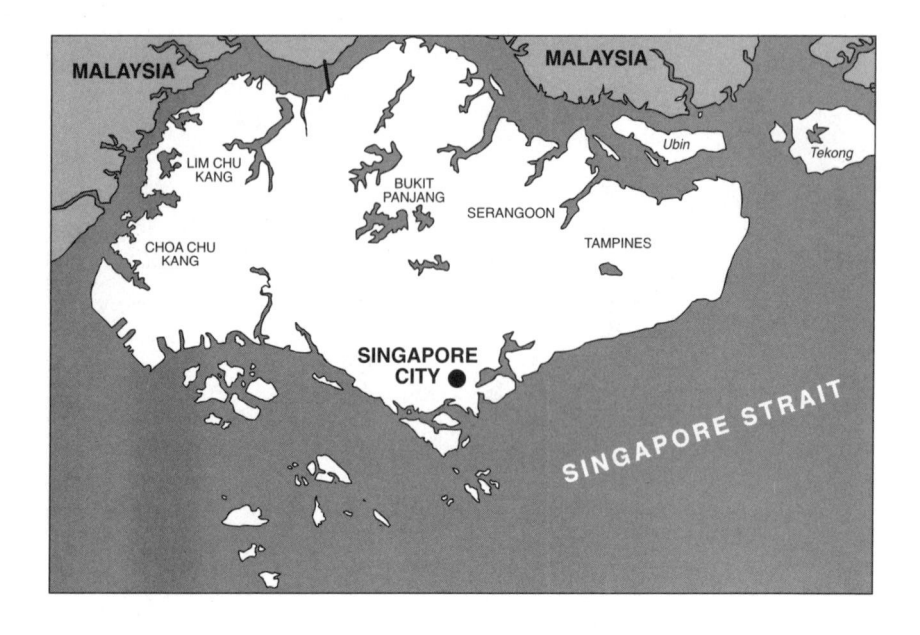

Thailand

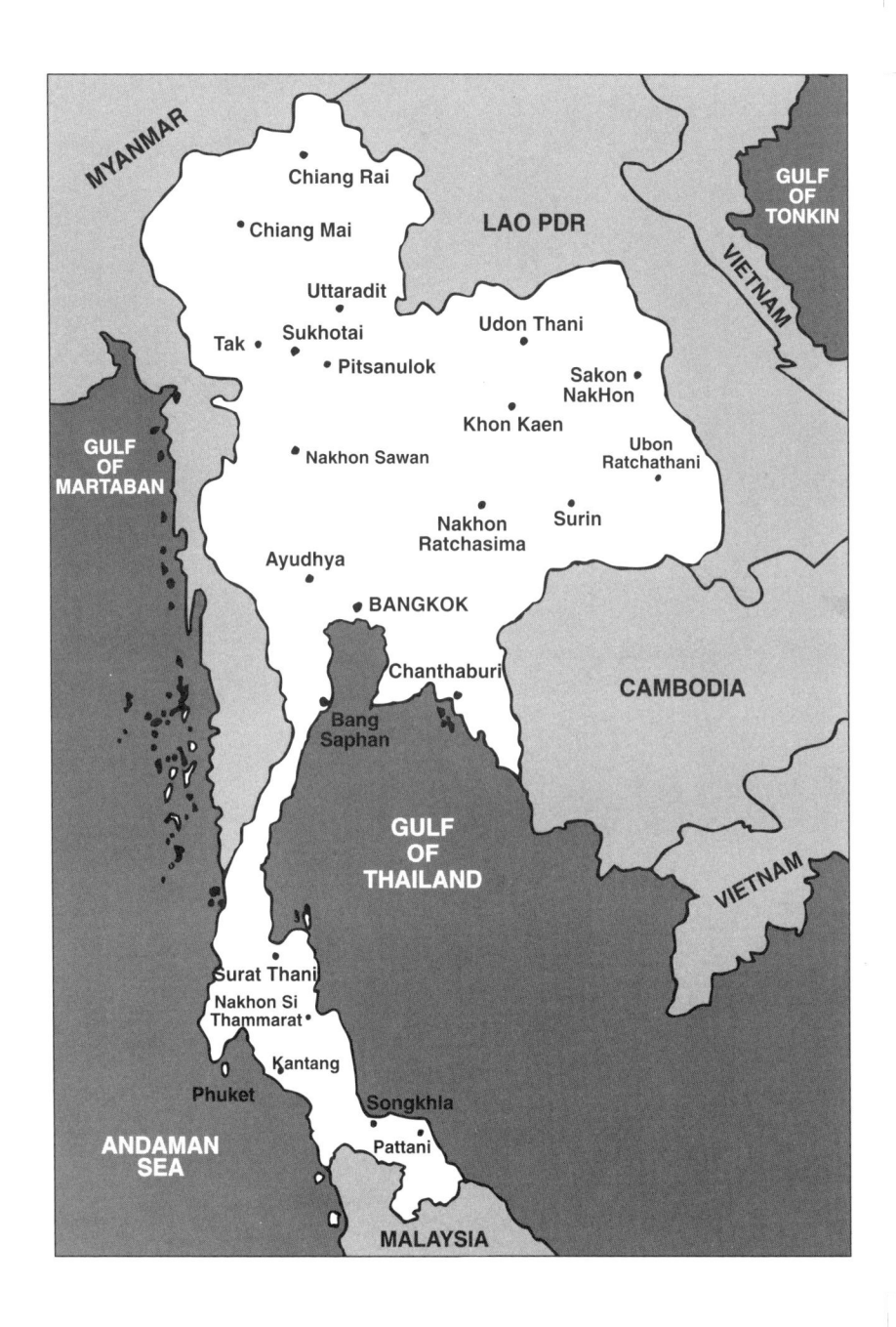

Vietnam

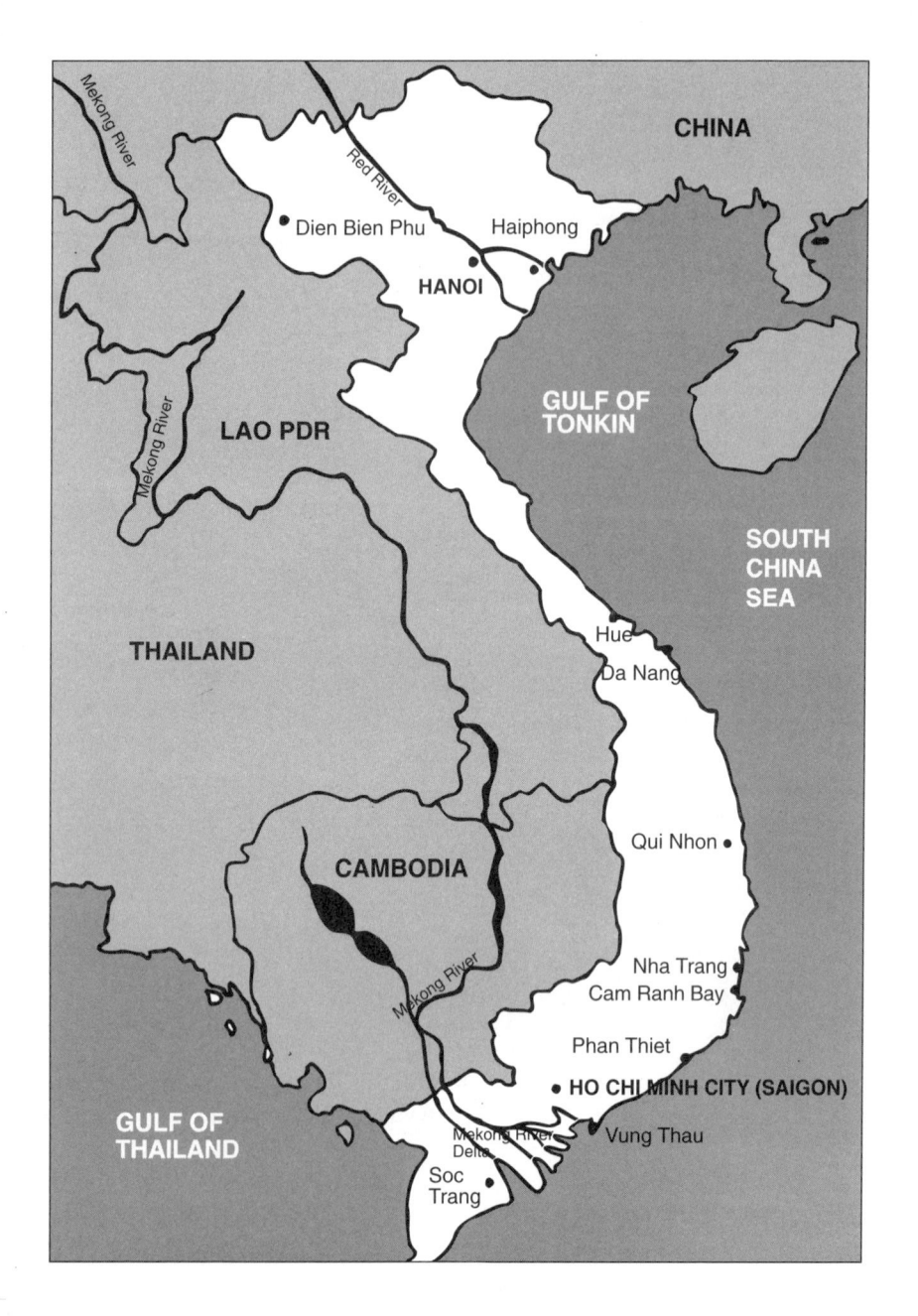

About the Asean Focus Group

Asean Focus Group is targeted at the business opportunities which lie in the six member countries of the Association of South East Asean Nations – ASEAN namely: Brunei Darussalam, Indonesia, Malaysia, Philippines, Singapore and Thailand.

We also increasingly work elsewhere in Asia such as the emerging markets of Vietnam, Lao, Cambodia, Myanmar, China and India.

Asean Focus Group is a well established player in the markets of Southeast Asia. Our executives have spent most of their professional careers involved with the region, recognising many years ago the importance and potential of what is now the most dynamic economic growth area of the world.

The Group's long term commitment to the region is manifest in its desire to act as an investor in appropriate growth businesses in Southeast Asia.

Our focussed commitment to our clients is established at the outset of the development of any business relationship as we only work with one company in any particular business sector.

The Asean Focus Group:

- advises a number of major companies operating or seeking to operate in the region across a broad range of activities including manufacturing, food processing, construction, finance, transportation and distribution, law and accounting

- acts as a project developer in the region and is currently involved in projects covering major areas of infrastructure development such as power, water and ports as well as other important sectors such as health and education

- invests in selected greenfield and existing joint ventures throughout the Asian region.

ASEAN FOCUS GROUP PTY LTD

LEVEL 10, 76-80 CLARENCE STREET, SYDNEY, NSW 2000 AUSTRALIA

Bangkok, Canberra, Hanoi, Hong Kong, Jakarta, Kuala Lumpur,
New Delhi, Singapore, Sydney and Yangon